MY CELL PHONE CAN THINK:

A Textbook on Artificial Intelligence

MICHIRO NEGISHI

DEDICATION

This book is dedicated to children with curious minds to whom the future belongs.

CONTENTS

ACKNOWLEDGMENTS

When I was in elementary school, my hobby was to make crystal radio receivers. As the years passed, I became obsessed with the philosophy of thinking. My interest in Artificial Intelligence sparked on a hot summer day in Japan while I was walking to my college when I suddenly realized that my thoughts could be simulated on a computer by simulating neural activities. As a part of my interests, I read about Frank Rosenblatt's perceptron, John Hopfield's associative memory, Kunihiko Fukushima's neocognitron, and Shun-ichi Amari's mathematical analysis of neural networks.

I would like to specially thank Professor Hiroshi Kawarada from Tokyo Institute of Technology, Professor Stephen Grossberg and Professor Daniel Bullock from Boston University, and Professor Jose Hanson from Rutgers University for supporting my work on neural modeling of pattern recognition and child language acquisition.

I would like to thank my wife Meena Negishi and my children Kanta and Seiji Negishi, without whose support this book would not have been possible.

1 WHAT IS ARTIFICIAL INTELLIGENCE?

1.1 Artificial intelligence everywhere

Machines are getting smarter. Cell phones can organize pictures by recognizing your family's faces. Computers can translate sentences from a Spanish website into English. Increasingly, the chatbot on your cell phone understand what you say and can play music or answer your questions (Figure 1.1). Computers can help doctors make diagnoses (Figure 1.2). There are robots that understand emotions (Figure 1.3), and some cars can even drive without drivers (Figure 1.4). It seems like these machines can think and act like humans. How do they do it?

Figure 1.1 Talking to a chatbot on the cell phone.

You may already know that these machines come with "smart" computer programs. While humans made these programs, they didn't program them to act in specific ways in specific situations. Instead, these computer programs can learn from and react to new situations. These machines are based on artificial intelligence (AI) technology. The beginning of AI dates back to the mid-1900s. In fact, AI is almost as old as the origin of computer programs. The mathematician Alan Turing gave a lot of thought to what computer programs could and couldn't do (Turing 1938) [9] and also developed the "Turing Test" to decide whether a machine could really be called intelligent. Computer scientist John McCarthy is believed to have coined the term "Artificial Intelligence" in 1956.

Figure 1.2 Computers are helping doctors to diagnose diseases.

What is AI? Let's start with a standard answer. According to Wikipedia, AI is "intelligence demonstrated by machines, in contrast to the natural intelligence displayed by humans and other animals" (retrieved 9/13/2018). But then we must define intelligence, do we not? This book adopts the following definition of AI: "AI is the capability of a machine to acquire knowledge from experience and apply it, generating behaviors in new situations." This often implies that the situations and behaviors must be complex enough to require "intelligence," meaning that AI is often a moving target. For example, something that used to be called AI, such as task scheduling, may no longer be called AI because these tasks are no longer considered complex.

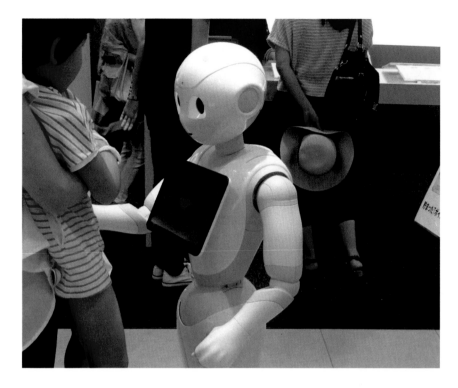

Figure 1.3 Robots aren't science fiction anymore.

Before AI, computers were programmed to perform exact tasks. For example, "If you are driving at 40 mph and the signal turns yellow, apply mild braking." This meant that humans had to program computers with all the necessary knowledge for them to work in any possible situation. Sometimes, this was really hard. For computers to be more flexible, computer systems needed input to determine which situations they were in. For that, they needed eyes (cameras), ears (microphones), and other sensors. In some cases, the input is simply a traditional computer keyboard, where we type natural English sentences instead of a pre-defined set of commands. Computer systems also have output devices, such as voice synthesizers and graphics displays. Then comes the complex part between the inputs and outputs: the thinking part. It wasn't enough for computers to do exactly what they were told in predetermined situations. To cope with new situations, computers must generalize from what they are told and what they experience. Three main components of AI can tackle this, "I can't tell you everything beforehand" problem: logic, statistics, and artificial neural networks (ANNs).

Figure 1.4 Autonomous cars can drive themselves with little supervision from human drivers.

1.2 Logic

The first component of AI we'll consider is logic, which is a method of using facts and rules to decide on the truth of statements. Logic has a very long history. Earlier than 300 BC, the Greek philosopher Aristotle developed a formal system for inferring things. For example, from the following two statements—"Candies are sweet," and "A lollipop is a candy"—you can infer that "A lollipop is sweet." This is a form of inference called syllogism. Another often-cited example is, "All humans are mortal," and "Socrates is a human;" therefore, "Socrates dies" (Figure 1.5). These are simple applications of a system of logic called predicate logic.

Figure 1.5 A dialogue with Aristotle, a philosopher who developed a classic system of logic.

Other logical systems can express logical relations, such as necessity and probability (modal logic), or time (temporal logic). Also, instead of treating all logical relations as one global system, sub-worlds can be defined to apply local rules. These can be used to build intelligent programs because logic can infer new facts from already known facts and rules, which is called deduction. Logical systems can also learn by generating rules from known facts, which is called induction and is the opposite of deduction. With advanced logical formulations, machines can do incredibly complex things, such as designing computer chips, monitoring power plants, proving logical theorems, and solving mathematical equations. At some point, researchers thought we might be able to store all necessary knowledge on a computer in a logical form, allowing the computer to think. In 1982, an ambitious project for developing logic-based AI systems, called the Fifth Generation Computer Project, began in Japan. This project produced fast inference machines but failed to make a significant impact in the world of information processing. One of the problems with logic-based AI is that a lot of commonsense knowledge is required to make inferences the way humans do, and it's almost impossible to gather a sufficient amount of this knowledge. Another problem is that that the computer must know the real-world meaning of words, which are arbitrary labels for real-world things and events, to make useful guesses. For example, the computer has to know how chocolate is related not only to sweetness and the color brown but also to Valentine's Day and even to dentists. Another problem is that simple symbolic logic does not work well when things are uncertain, such as tomorrow's weather or throwing dice.

1.3 Statistics

Statistics, the second component of AI, deals with uncertainties. Statistics talks about the probability of something happening. For example, you may think that you have more headaches on rainy days. This is relevant to AI because it can be used to infer the likelihood of one event given another event. This kind of dependence of events is described concisely by Bayes' rule, named after a statistician, Reverend Thomas Bayes (Figure 1.6). Another simple example would be making guesses about your classmates. Imagine Mark is a smart fifth grader who wears glasses, and that he thinks students who wear glasses are smart. To prove he's right, he first has to define smartness. Then, he has to count four groups of students: students who wear glasses and are smart, students who wear glasses and are not smart, students without glasses who are smart, and, finally, students without glasses who are not smart. He can't only include his friends, because his group of friends may not be a good sample of all possible students. He can be surer of his statistics when he includes his entire class, grade, or school. By using statistics, you can compute the probabilities of facts based on conditions that you know. Statistics may help you to say with some certainty that if A wears glasses, A is likely to be smart.

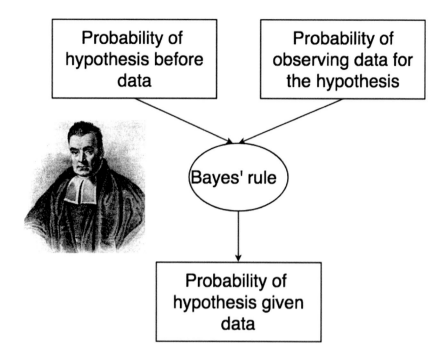

Figure 1.6 Application of Bayes' rule, which is one of the basic rules in statistics.

For a more concrete example of statistical inference, think about a candy dispenser that either gives you an orange or a melon gumball every time you turn a knob. Suppose that 70% of the gumballs are melon, but you like the taste of the orange gumballs better. In this case, you will be unhappy 70% of the time if you keep getting gumballs. But if there are two gumball machines and you know that one of them has 70% melon and 30% orange gumballs, whereas the other machine has 70% orange and 30% melon gumballs, you can develop an intelligent strategy. After one machine keeps giving you more melon than orange gumballs, you might conclude that it is the 70% melon machine and switch to the other. How many gumballs do you need to get before deciding whether to switch to the machine with more orange-flavored gumballs? You can answer this question if you learn statistics. Statistics is a big bag of tools you can use to infer the underlying structure that explains the data. Once you infer the structure, you can use that inference to decide on the best action to take given your observations.

Statistics is an important part of AI. The strength of statistics lies in its rigorous mathematical formulation. A good thing about statistics is, once you reach a conclusion about what to do, it's possible to explain how you reached that conclusion and your degree of certainty about whether your conclusion is correct. However, this is sometimes a double-edged sword because people tend to prefer clarity, which requires a simple hypothesized structure. But the pursuit for simplicity can get in the way of the best results. Also, finding the best underlying structure becomes increasingly difficult in complex situations.

1.4 Artificial neural networks

Another way to make a computer think like a human is to make programs that work like the human brain. But how does the human brain work? The brain is amazing. It makes you feel, think, and move. A human brain is made of 100 billion tiny cells called neurons. That's more than ten times the number of people on the Earth. Imagine ten times the people on earth holding hands with each other. That's your brain. Best of all, the brain learns by changing the way neurons are interconnected. Neurons line up in thin layers of sheets like newspapers. In fact, the size of the sheet of neurons in your brain is about at the size of a newspaper. But wait, how does a newspaper fit in your brain? By crumpling, of course. That's why your brain has lots of wrinkles.

Each neuron has (1) inputs that collect signals from other neurons, (2) a decision-making section that determines how it reacts to these inputs, and (3) an output that sends out its decision (Figure 1.7). The input section of a neuron is made up of dendrites, which look like branches and trees. The processing unit is the fat part of the neuron at the center, called the cell body, which gathers all the inputs and decides how and when to send out a signal. The output is called the axon, which is a cable that transmits the signal decided on by the cell body to all the surrounding, interconnected neurons. The connection between the axon and the dendrite is called a synapse.

8

How does a neuron learn? By changing the strengths of its connections. The strength of a connection is called a connection weight or a synaptic weight.

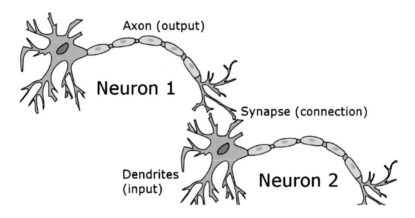

Figure 1.7 The basic elements making up your brain, are called neurons, or nerve cells.

Inspired by the way neurons work, scientists created the Artificial Neural Network (ANN, Figure 1.8, right). ANNs are some of the most important components of the AI that allows machines to learn from experience. Like humans, ANNs get smarter by learning from examples. We still don't know all the details about how the connection weights of the brain's neurons are changed, but scientists have developed useful ways of changing the connection weights in ANNs each time they process incoming data. For example, each time an ANN is presented with a different face, the connection weights are changed slightly, so the ANN gets better at differentiating faces, while also identifying the faces of the same person. Or, in the case of translating sentences on a website, the ANN is presented with sentences in Spanish, and the weights are changed gradually after the presentation of each sentence so that the outputs will be closer and closer to the desired English sentences.

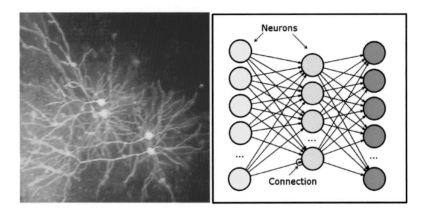

Figure 1.8 Biological (left) and artificial (right) neural networks.

There are three ways you can learn at school. The first is to learn from a teacher who will give you a question and the correct answer. The second is to learn without a teacher by simply observing what you see, hear, etc. The third is to do and learn—to act and observe the outcome. These are the three ways ANNs can learn things, too. The first way, learning with a teacher who tells you the answer, is called supervised learning (Chapter 3). Supervised learning neural networks are given training data and then compute an output, which they compare to the desired output provided by the teacher. Then they change the connection weights to make the output closer to the desired output. The second way, learning without a teacher, is called unsupervised learning (Chapter 4). In unsupervised learning, the ANN is given a lot of examples. Then it tries to figure out how the data can be organized. The third way, learning from a teacher who lets you try and then tells you how well you did, is called reinforcement learning (Chapter 5).

Each type of learning has strengths and weaknesses. Supervised learning is very effective but requires that all input data are paired with correct answers. With unsupervised learning, the ANN doesn't need to be given the correct answers, but it's not possible to learn everything this way. For instance, it's hard to learn multiplication through self-organization. Reinforcement learning takes a long time, but sometimes it's the only way you can learn. For example, when playing a board game, you don't receive feedback about the correct answer every time you make a move.

There are also ANN learning algorithms that are rooted in a branch of physics called thermodynamics. These algorithms include the Hopfield network and the Boltzmann machine. An American physicist, John Hopfield, developed the Hopfield network. Ludwig Boltzmann did not invent the Boltzmann machine – he was an Austrian physicist in the 19th to early 20th centuries. When the Hopfield network or the Boltzmann machine runs, the activation pattern (imagine a pattern of shining stars where highly active neurons correspond to bright stars) of the neurons changes over time to make a single value – called the energy – smaller. The energy of an ANN is defined by the activation pattern and the connection weights. The energy of the network decreases as the activity pattern changes, just like potential energy decreases as a ball goes down a hill. Boltzmann developed an equation that relates the energy associated with a pattern to the probability that a system ends up in that pattern. The main difference between the Hopfield network and the Boltzmann machine is that some noise (a random variation) is added to the neural activities in the Boltzmann machine. This means that the Boltzmann machine has a jumpier ball that may take more time to settle, but it may eventually settle into a better (lower energy) state than the Hopfield network. These networks can be used in a wide range of applications. For instance, they can recall memories given incomplete data, such as an image with added noise or missing pixels. In our definitions, the Hopfield network and the Boltzmann machine are classified as unsupervised learning networks, since they do not involve a teacher. However, they are sometimes classified as supervised methods because the Hopfield network and the Boltzmann machine can be configured as though they are standard supervised learning networks. Also, unlike other unsupervised learning methods, they typically do not develop easy-to-interpret internal representations.

All three components of AI—logic, statistics, and ANN—are important and are often used in combination to make computers intelligent. Recent developments in AI have a lot to do with rapid progress made in the research and applications of ANNs, which this book focuses on.

Questions

2. What are the three components of AI?

3. What are the cells in the brain that are used for thinking called?

4. What are the connections between the cells in the brain called?

5. The sum of three angles of any triangle is 180 degrees. A right triangle is a triangle. What can you conclude from these?

Answers

1. Logic, statistics, and ANNs; 2. Neurons; 3. Synapses; 4. The sum of the three angles of a right triangle is 180 degrees.

2 THE DEVELOPMENT OF ARTIFICIAL NEURAL NETWORKS

2.1 The beginning

Before the development of ANNs, scientists needed to understand at least some aspects of the brain's neural networks. Maybe we shouldn't go as far back in history as the time when Greek philosophers hypothesized that the brain was merely a cooling apparatus. Even after people started investigating the microstructures in the brain, it took a while before they discovered that the brain was a network of neurons. The concept of the "neuron," like those of electrons and protons, wasn't popular, at first. The reticular theory, which claimed that the nervous system was a continuous network, had been quite popular. The reticular theory was advocated by physician Camillo Golgi (1843–1926), who invented a groundbreaking method for observing the nervous system. Thus, the neuron doctrine, which postulated neurons were discrete building blocks, had to fight against the reticular theory. The neuron doctrine owes a lot to neuroscientist Santiago Ramon y Cajal (1852–1934), who made meticulous observations of the microstructure of the nervous system. Interestingly, Golgi and Cajal shared a Nobel Prize in 1906, which prolonged the conflict between the two parties.

The first people who thought each neuron could act as a logic gate and that it could be combined to form a complex computing system were McCulloch and Pitts (Figure 2.1) (1943)[6]. McCulloch was a neurophysiologist, and Pitts was a logician, an ideal combination. In fact, McCulloch, an established scholar, took in Pitts, who was somewhat of a prodigy. A neuron is an incredibly complex organ, involving a myriad of sub-processes from the molecular to cellular levels. At a very abstract level, a neuron can be understood as an electronic device that receives inputs from other neurons, weighs and accumulates them, and decides whether or not to produce an output (Figure 2.1). McCulloch and Pitts realized that neurons might function like the logic gates that are used in computer chips. Think of a simple artificial neuron with two inputs and one output. Assume the inputs and the output are OFF (0) or ON (1). Also assume that all input weights are 1 (in other words, all inputs are simply added before processing). If the function that decides the output is, "If the sum of inputs is equal to or above 2, then the output is ON; otherwise, the output is OFF," then the artificial neuron acts as an AND gate (Figure 2.1, right top)—if both inputs are ON, then the output is ON.

On the other hand, if the output rule is, "If the weighted sum is equal to or above 1, then the output is ON; otherwise, the output is OFF," then the artificial neuron acts as an OR gate (Figure 2.1, right middle)—the output is ON only when at least one input is ON. We can also make a NOT gate if we change the assumption slightly. In a NOT gate, there is only one input, and the rule is, "If the input is ON, then the output is OFF, and if the input is ON, then the output is OFF." To make a NOT gate (Figure 2.1, right bottom), an artificial neuron would have only one input, with a weight of negative one, and the output rule would be, "If the weighted input is equal to or above 0, the output is ON; otherwise, the output is OFF." By combining these artificial neurons, you can build any complex computer you want, although theoretically you only need one type of neuron that computes a logic operation called NAND (Not-AND) to build any logic circuits. As of 2018, a state-of-the-art central processing unit (CPU) has hundreds of thousands of logic gates (about 1.5 million transistors at 3 transistors per gate).

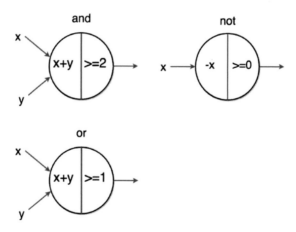

Figure 2.1 Modeling the neurons. Upper left: Warren Pitts (a logician, right) and Jerome Levin (cognitive scientist, left). Upper right: Warren McCulloch. Lower: McCulloch and Pitts model neurons configured as AND, OR, and NOT gates (see text).

Figure 2.2. Frank Rosenblatt, creator of the perceptron. The perceptron is a mechanism that executes a supervised neural network learning algorithm.

Although you can build any complex logic this way, this isn't the end of the story for developing intelligent machines. Intelligent machines must also be able to learn, just like the human brain does.

Without the ability to learn, even a supercomputer needs someone to program it, which isn't intelligence. The first learning theory traces back to a psychologist, Donald Hebb. In his book *The Organization of Behavior* (1949)[2], Hebb said, "When an axon of cell A is near enough to excite a cell B and repeatedly or persistently takes part in firing it, some growth process or metabolic change takes place in one or both cells such that A's efficiency, as one of the cells firing B, is increased." This is a fancy way of saying that when two neurons get excited together, the connection weights between them increase. Although simple, this was a profound insight. The first ANN model with learning capability, called the perceptron, was developed by Frank Rosenblatt in 1957 [7] (Figures 2.2 and 2.3). Rosenblatt was a psychologist with a wide spectrum of interests, including biology. Though the perceptron was first implemented as a computer program, it was originally designed and was later realized as an image recognition machine, with 400 photocells as inputs and motor-controlled potentiometers (variable resistors) as adjustable connection weights.

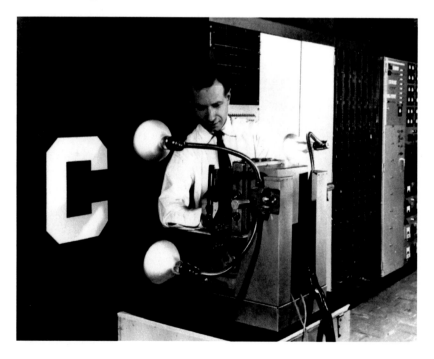

Figure 2.3 The Mark I perceptron.

2.2 The first neural networks winter

People were excited to see a system that mimicked the human visual system. It also created a lot of hype, such as the idea that someday machines like the perceptron would develop their own consciousness and control humans. However, the machine's limitations soon became apparent. The biggest problem was that Rosenblatt could not come up with an effective algorithm for adjusting the weights in the intermediate layer neurons; that is, the neurons that weren't directly connected to the output. While it was easy to adjust the weights to the output to reduce errors, there were no effective ways to adjust the weights in earlier layers. This and other factors, including Minsky's influential book (see Box 2.1), tipped the balance of the research trend within the AI research community and led to the first neural networks winter, or downfall, in the 1970s.

2.3 The second neural networks boom

Attention returned to ANNs when several people found ways to train multiple layer neural networks through a technique called backpropagation (Figure 2.4). Many aspects of the backpropagation algorithm were developed by different researchers, including Kelley, Bryson, Linnainmaa, Werbos, and Dreyfus. Using the backpropagation algorithm, ANNs with multiple layers could be trained to yield outputs closer to the desired output values (see Chapter 3 for more details about backpropagation). With the backpropagation algorithm, people were encouraged to test ANNs in many application areas, and the research flourished. In cognitive science, neural network modeling shed new and sometimes controversial insights into perceptual and cognitive processes.

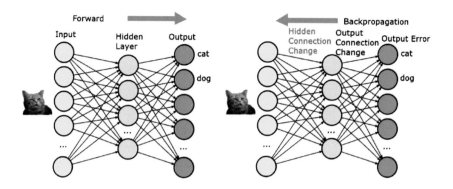

Figure 2.4 The backpropagation algorithm. Backpropagation provides an effective way to change hidden connections to reduce output errors.

2.4 The second neural networks winter

Training ANNs takes a lot of computation, and computing power was limited in the era when backpropagation was developed. Thus, ANN applications were limited to small data, sometimes called "toy problems." However, it turned out that with small data and small networks, the results of ANNs could not compete with sophisticated, statistics-based algorithms. In fact, multilayer ANNs with backpropagation were framed as a specific type of statistical method that iteratively improve parameters. In the engineering world, including image and speech recognition, people were interested in how good the results were, not in how the method was related to human intelligence or to neuroscience. Thus, people became less interested in neural network research, which led to a second winter of neural networks research in the 1990s.

2.5 The third neural networks boom

Nevertheless, some researchers persevered in experimenting and improving the techniques in neural networks research. These researchers included Geoffrey Hinton and Yann LeCun, just to name a few (Figure 2.5). LeCun continued research into applying ANNs in the field of pattern recognition. His ANNs often involved many layers, some of which had local, shared-weight connections; these were sometimes called convolutional neural networks. Similarly,

Geoffrey Hinton continued to advance basic algorithms. He also teamed up with other scientists, like Yann LeCun and Joshua Bengio, to establish research initiatives and receive funding, which was a hard task. Then, something interesting happened. The speed of the type of computing that ANNs required (single-instruction-multiple-data computing) was vastly accelerated by graphics processing units (GPUs), which had been developed to increase the speed of computer games, among other purposes (Figure 2.6). As you probably know, the basic components of computers become more powerful every year. Moore's law states that the number of transistors on computer chips doubles every two years. With faster computers, it became possible to train ANN models with more complex structures with huge amounts of data. People realized that the limitations in the quality of ANN results weren't really due to the limitations of the algorithms but to the computing power and amount of data available. In other words, with more computing power, people felt free to experiment with building more complex models with more layers (thus the name "deep learning"). Combined with some improvements in the algorithms (including those utilized new output functions for neurons and those that randomly disable neurons), ANN began to beat the outcomes of the statistical methods (LeCun et al. 2015)[5].

Figure 2.5 Some of the people who have contributed to the current resurgence in neural networks (from left: Geoffrey Hinton, Yann LeCun, Joshua Bengio, and Andrew Ng).

Many people are rightly concerned about the current state of ANNs. First, unlike logic and statistics, it's difficult to interpret what ANNs are doing. Although people often care more about the quality of results than their interpretability, sometimes this lack of transparency raises safety concerns, such as if the machine is operating a car. For some applications, humans must interact with the machines, in which case, the machine should be able to account for its actions. Second, ANNs don't always generalize when they encounter inputs different from those they are trained on. As such, interpretability and generalizability are active research areas in ANNs.

Figure 2.6 Graphics processing units can be used to speed up neural computation.

Box 2.1 Season changes in artificial intelligence

The "neural network winter" is often attributed to the book *Perceptron* written by Minsky and Papert in 1969, which explained how neural networks with only local connections can't compute certain functions. It's often claimed, incorrectly, that Minksy and Papert also conjectured that not even multiple-layer perceptrons would be able to implement an Exclusive OR (XOR) gate. Minsky obviously knew that multilayer perceptrons could implement any logical circuit. True or not, many people believe this book changed the tide in the AI research and caused the neural network winter. During that period, AI research was dominated by logic (symbol processing). When symbolic AI couldn't deliver what it promised, it brought down the whole field.

Figure 2.7 Minsky and Papert's book *Perceptron* published in 1969 analyzed the class of computations that multilayer perceptrons could and could not achieve.

Questions

1. McCulloch and Pitts found what to be like the basic building block that can be used to build any complex logical circuits?

2. Who said, "When an axon of cell A is near enough to excite a cell B and repeatedly or persistently takes part in firing it, some growth process or metabolic change takes place in one or both cells such that A's efficiency, as one of the cells firing B, is increased?"

3. What is increased in the above statement? The input, the output, or the connection strength?

4. What is the algorithm that contributed to the end of the first neural network winter?

Answers

1. Neuron; 2. Donald Hebb; 3. The connection strength;
4. Backpropagation.

3 ARTIFICIAL NEURAL NETWORKS THAT LEARN FROM TEACHERS

3.1 Supervised learning: learning from a teacher

A supervised learning ANN learns from a teacher (Figure 3.1). First, the network receives some form of input, such as visual or auditory input, and produces some output, such as the answer to whether the input was from a cat or a dog (Figure 3.2). The network is then given the correct answer from a teacher so it can adjust its connection weights to arrive at correct answers. As you can imagine, it's easier to learn with a teacher than it is to learn by simply reading textbooks. On the other hand, you always need a good teacher beside you.

Figure 3.1 A teacher provides the correct answers in supervised learning.

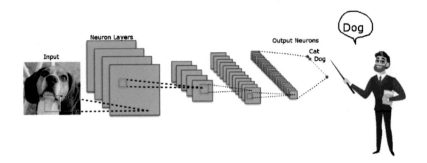

Figure 3.2 A convoluted deep-learning network in a supervised learning setting.

Let's look at a simple network with a team of two artificial neurons, one specialized in finding the letter x, and the other specialized in finding the symbol +. This is one team or a one-layer network. The input is made of nine plates arranged in a 3 x 3 square (Figure 3.3). Each artificial neuron has nine input hands touching the input plates, and each artificial neuron is also a "pass-through" that weighs inputs and sends outputs directly without further processing. This is an example of a single-layer (one team), linear (pass-through) ANN model.

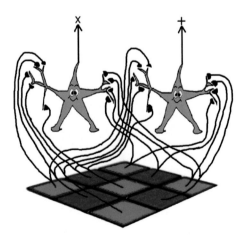

Figure 3.3 A single-layer artificial neural network. The output layer consists of two artificial neurons, each specializing in recognizing one symbol.

This network can learn to read the letter x and symbol + using the delta rule. The delta is a Greek character used in mathematics to symbolize a small change. The small delta looks a little like number 6 (δ), and a capital delta looks like a triangle (Δ). The delta rule for linear artificial neurons is:

Change of weight = small constant * desired change * input
Desired change = target - output

(Note: an asterisk means multiplication in formulas in this book).

In the above equation, each time a network is presented with an input data, each connection weight is changed by the product of three terms. The first term is a small constant, such as 0.01. The second term is the desired change, that is, the amount of change required for the output to become the correct value. In the following, we'll see an example of how the weight change by the delta rule brings the output closer to the desired output.

3.2 Computing the output

Let's compute this output in a small example where we want to distinguish the letter "x" from the symbol "+". For simplicity, our inputs are:

$$
\text{Input "x"} = \begin{matrix} 101 \\ 010 \\ 101 \end{matrix} \qquad \text{Input "+"} = \begin{matrix} 010 \\ 111 \\ 010 \end{matrix}
$$

The first formula simply means the input corresponding to the letter 'X' consists of darkness at the nine sections of the square, "1,0,1,0,1,0,1,0,1." The target value for the "x" artificial neuron is 1.0 when the input is x and 0 when the input is +. Let's assume that the weights are all 0.01. It's not usual to set all the weights the same, but it helps us see how the weights change in this simple network. If we arrange the weights according to the input plate positions, the weight pattern of the artificial neurons looks like this:

0.0100 0.0100 0.0100
0.0100 0.0100 0.0100
0.0100 0.0100 0.0100

Then, the output of the "x" artificial neuron for the input "x" is:

output for x = sum of input * weight for each input plate

$$= 1 \times 0.01 + 0 \times 0.01 + 1 * 0.01 +$$
$$0 \times 0.01 + 1 \times 0.01 + 0 \times 0.01 +$$
$$1 \times 0.01 + 0 \times 0.01 + 1 \times 0.01$$

$$= 0.01 + 0.0 + 0.01 + 0.0 + 0.01 + 0.0 + 0.01 + 0.0 + 0.01$$

$$= 0.05 \text{ (Figure 3.4 (1))}$$

3.3 Comparing the output to the desired output

For this data ("x"), the input to the first connection of the "x" neuron is 1 (the top left corner), and it is desired that the output of the neuron will change from 0.05 to 1.0.

desired change * input

$$= \text{(target - output)} * \text{input}$$

$$= (1.0 - 0.05) * 1$$

$$= 0.95 * 1$$

$$= 0.95$$

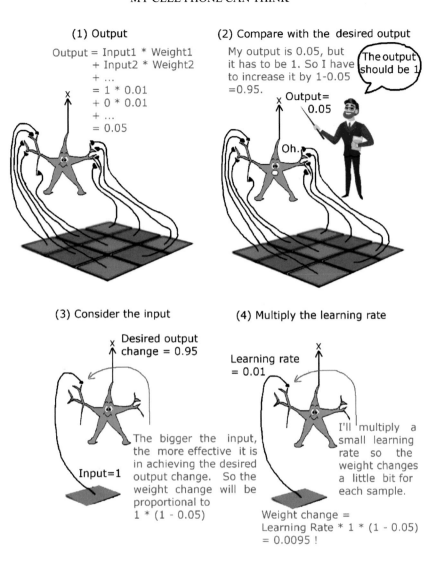

Figure 3.4 Learning by the delta rule.

3.4 Changing the connection weight

How do we change the weights so that the output gets closer to 1.0? For a weight that gets input 1 (Figure 3.3(3)), the output approaches 1 by increasing the weight. You can see that the increment depends on both the input and the desired change: as long as the input is positive, a positive weight change brings the output closer to the desired value if the desired change is positive. If the desired change is negative, then the weight should be decreased. If the input is 0, changing the weight does not affect the output. If the input is negative, the direction of the weight change direction should be flipped. For example, if the input is -1, the weight should be decreased if the desired change is positive. One way to accomplish this is to change the weight proportional to the product of the input and the desired change (Figure 3.3(3)).

In practice, we should change the weight slowly, so the weights are adjusted little by little for each input. Thus, we multiply a small constant called the learning constant, which, in our case, is 0.01 (Figure 3.3(4)).

Weight change

= learning constant * (desired change * input)

= 0.01 * 0.95 * 1

= 0.0095

So the first weight will be increased by 0.0095 and become 0.0195. It is the same for all other weights whose input plates have the value of 1, because we assumed that they initially had the same weights.

For input plates whose value was 0, the weight change will be:

learning constant * desired change * input

= learning constant * (target - output) * input

= 0.01 * (1.0 - 0.05) * 0

= 0.01 * 0.95 * 0

= 0.0

So, these weights stay the same. As a result, the weight pattern of the "x" artificial neuron will be:

```
0.0195  0.0100  0.0195
0.0100  0.0195  0.0100
0.0195  0.0100  0.0195
```

After this weight change, the output to the letter x will be

= 1 x 0.0195 + 0 x 0.0100 + 1 * 0.0195 +
  0 x 0.0100 + 1 x 0.0195 + 0 x 0.0100 +
  1 x 0.0195 + 0 x 0.0100 + 1 x 0.0195

= 0.0196 + 0.0 + 0.0195 + 0.0 + 0.0195 + 0.0 + 0.0195 + 0.0 +
  0.0195

= 0.0975

Remember that before the weight change, the output was 0.05. Thus, the output increased, bringing it closer to the correct output that is 1.0.

Now, we shift our attention to the "+" artificial neuron. Because the initial weights were the same as those for the "x" artificial neuron, the initial output for "x" was the same as that for the "x" artificial neuron, 0.05.

But the target for this artificial neuron is 0, so the weight change of the first weight will be:

learning constant * desired change * input

= learning constant * (target - output) * input

= 0.01 * (0.0 - 0.05) * 1

= 0.01 * (-0.05) * 1

= -0.0005

and the change is the same for all weights whose input is 1. So, these weights will change to 0.01 - 0.0005 = 0.0095. The weight change for all weights whose input is 0 will be:

learning constant * desired change * input = 0

With these weight changes, the weights for the "+" artificial neuron will be:

0.0095 0.0100 0.0095
0.0100 0.0095 0.0100
0.0095 0.0100 0.0095

and the output of this artificial neuron for the input "x" will decrease from 0.05 to

0.0095 + 0.0 + 0.0095 + 0.0 + 0.0095 +0.0 + 0.0095 + 0.0 +
    0.0095

= 0.0475

As such, the output of the "x" artificial neuron in response to "x" was increased, and the output of the "+" artificial neuron in response to "x" was decreased.

Next, the network is trained for the symbol +. This will decrease the output of the "x" artificial neuron and increase the output of the

"+" artificial neuron in response to the input "+," but unfortunately it will also negate the learning for the input "x" to some degree. The way ANNs work is to train the network for both samples of "x" and samples of "+" alternatingly and repeatedly. After many iterations of learning, the output of the "x" artificial neuron in response to "x" becomes closer and closer to 1.0, and the output in response to "+" becomes closer and closer to 0.0; and the output of the "+" artificial neuron in response to "+" becomes closer and closer to 1.0, and the output in response to "x" becomes closer and closer to 0.0

Congratulations! You have now understood the delta rule, which is the first step towards understanding backpropagation, one of the most widely used algorithms in ANNs.

Questions

1. What four numbers do you require to determine the change of one connection in the delta rule?

2. How is the desired change of an neural output computed?

3. If there is more than one layer of artificial neurons—that is, if neurons are between the input and the output neurons—the method described in this chapter can't be used. Why not? Each artificial neuron has computable inputs and an output. What is missing?

4. If the supervised learning works, the weight change will become smaller and smaller. Why?

Answers

1. Input, output, desired output, and learning constant; 2. By subtracting the computed output from the desired output; 3. Desired outputs are not given for these "in between" neurons; 4. As the output becomes closer to the desired output, the desired change will become smaller.

Box 3.1. Neural net dreams

When we train an ANN with many layers of artificial neurons to recognize visual inputs, what does each layer learn? As it turns out, layers close to the input learn simple features, such as boundaries and lines, while layers closer to the output learn more integrated features, such as faces, flowers, and houses in the figures the network is trained on. Researchers have also developed ways for trained ANNs to generate, rather than recognize, images. They call this neural network daydreaming. The images created this way often have dream-like and sometimes scary qualities, as you can see in this image created by Martin Thoma, using Deep Dream Generator (deepdreamgenerator.com).

Figure 3.5 A picture generated by a generative neural network.

4 ARTIFICIAL NEURAL NETWORKS THAT LEARN FROM EXAMPLES

4.1 Unsupervised learning: learning without a teacher

In the previous chapter, we looked at supervised learning, which is a learning method that requires a teacher to tell the artificial neural network (ANN) what the correct answer is. This chapter looks at the opposite side—*unsupervised learning*—where ANNs learn by looking at examples, without being told what the examples are or how they should interpret them.

Figure 4.1 ANNs can learn to group apples and oranges in unsupervised learning.

For instance, ANNs are given images of apples and images of oranges without being told what these fruits are, and they learn to group them into apples and oranges (Figure 4.1). This is possible because the examples of apples are similar to each other just like the examples of oranges are similar to each other. In essence, the ANN has to learn what to pay attention to—in this case, probably colors and textures instead of sizes. These characteristics are called *features*. The ANN must learn to extract useful features from the images and to pay more attention to important features while ignoring unreliable ones. For example, features such as "round" and "shiny," are not as useful in this case, because all are. Note that features are selected NOT to distinguish apples and oranges – we do not have a teacher. Features are selected to make all the inputs widely different from each other.

4.2 Unsupervised ANNs that make maps

A well-known ANN model called the self-organizing feature map (SOFM) is an example of an unsupervised learning model (Kohonen 1982)[4]. The SOFM was invented by Teuvo Kohonen (Figure 4.2), a Finnish researcher in engineering. In the SOFM, similar inputs are placed in nearby locations on a neural map, and the inputs that are presented more frequently occupy more areas in the map. The more a specific type of input is seen, the more minute differences among the inputs belonging to that type are represented in the map. An SOFM is a cool tool for mapping any complex information on a sheet.

After all, your brain is made of neural sheets folded into your skull. In fact, a map with characteristics similar to those of an SOFM is found in the brain—the map of the human body. Located between the frontal and posterior parts of the brain, the primary sensory area is a two-dimensional map of the body, sometimes called the *homunculus* (a Latin word for "a small man;" see Figure 4.3). Like an SOFM, the primary sensory cortex preserves the topology of the body, but the relative area size of each part of the body is determined by how much that part is used. Because hands are used frequently, they are represented in large areas, and digits and parts of fingers are represented in small detail.

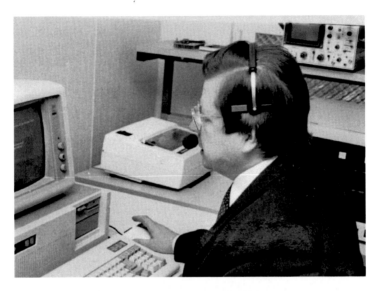

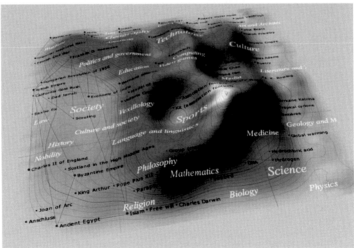

Figure 4.2 Teuvo Kohonen developed the self-organizing feature map (SOFM) model. The right figure shows a word map based on word frequencies appearing in Wikipedia.

Another example of a self-organized structure that emerges in the brain is the primary visual cortex (Figure 4.4). Neurophysiologists David Hubel and Torsten Wiesel (1974)[3]found a regular structure in the primary visual cortex containing subgroups of neurons sensitive to a particular orientation. This orientation changes slowly until it rotates fully, at which point, a new column starts that corresponds to the next small visual field (Figure 4.5). Hubel and Wiesel found that if one of a young cat's eyes is kept shut, the formation of the primary visual cortex is disrupted, indicating that the development of the primary visual cortex involves a self-organizing process.

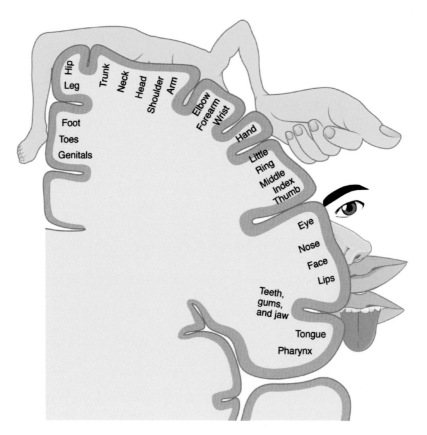

Figure 4.3 The sensory map of the body in the brain.

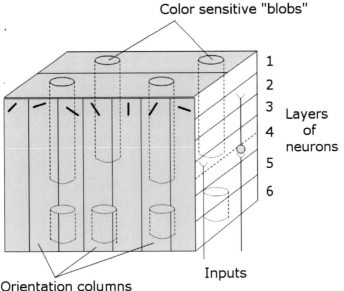

Figure 4.4 Hubel and Wiesel found visual columns in the cortex.

But how does the map appear on the neural sheet? To figure that out, let's consider how an SOFM learns by being exposed to input samples. During that exposure process, the SOFM learns to form neighborhoods, so that similar inputs activate nearby neurons. Initially, learning involves a large neighborhood; this neighborhood shrinks as the network learns more samples, assuming that inputs are the same size, meaning the sum of the squares of numbers in each input data is 1. Then, the training proceeds as follows:

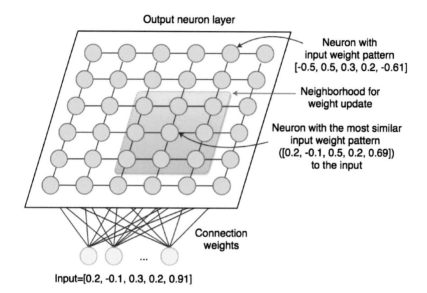

Figure 4.5 Self-organizing feature maps weight update.

1. We assume that neurons know nothing about inputs initially, so we set all the weights to small random values. To keep the explanation simple, let's assume that connections to one neuron are 0.2, –0.1, 0.5, 0.2, and 0.69. We write this set of connections in square brackets as [0.2, –0.1, 0.5, 0.2, 0.69]. There may be other neurons whose connections are [–0.5, 0.5, 0.3, 0.2, –0.61], and so on (Figure 4.5). The neighborhood size is initially set to a large value to cover all the neurons.

2. All neurons get activated by a new input pattern. The activations are computed by taking the weighted sum of the input, just as we did for supervised learning. For instance, if the input pattern is [0.2, –0.1, 0.3, 0.2, 0.91], the activation of the first neuron mentioned earlier (with weight [0.2, –0.1, 0.5, 0.2, 0.69]) will be 0.2 * 0.2 + (–0.1) * (–0.1) + 0.5 * 0.3 + 0.2 * 0.2 + 0.91 * 0.91 = 0.869.

3. Choose the neuron with the largest activation, and define the neighborhood within a radius "r" from that neuron. As it turns out, as long as the input data are of the same size as described above, and the weights are updated according to the rule described in step 4, a neuron with the weight pattern most similar to the input has the largest activation. In the current example, the first neuron wins because its connection pattern is closer to the input than the connection pattern of the second neuron.

4. Modify the weights of all the neurons in the neighborhood, so the weights yield larger activations. In the current case, all the weights of the neurons within "r" of the first neuron will be modified to be closer to the input pattern. All the weights of the neurons in the neighborhood are changed similarly.

5. Slightly reduce the neighborhood size and connection weight modification rate.

6. Go back to step 2. Repeat.

Initially, the weights are random, so neurons win by chance, but because the neighborhood covers the whole neural plane, it doesn't matter who wins—all input weights are changed to get closer to the inputs. The input weights to all neurons will approach the same pattern initially, which is the average of all the input patterns. When an input is given, some neurons respond strongly because their random weight patterns are closer to the input than the other neurons. Then, their weight patterns, along with the weights of the neurons near them, will be modified so the weight patterns will be closer to the input pattern. As the neighborhood area starts to shrink, some specialization of different areas occurs.

4.3 Unsupervised ANNs that make groups

We saw that an SOFM can create a map of inputs. Another thing an unsupervised learning neural network can do is group similar inputs (Figure 4.6). Grouping is also called *clustering, classification,* or *categorization,* with sometimes-varying definitions.

Figure 4.6 Grouping of images.

One example of a neural network that performs grouping is the adaptive resonance theory 1 (ART1) created by cognitive scientists Stephen Grossberg (Figure 4.7) and a mathematician, Gail Carpenter (Carpenter and Grossberg 1987)[1]. ART1 is designed to form stable memories by creating "resonance" (Figure 4.8) between two flows of data, (1) bottom-up activation from the input and (2) top-down activation (expectation) from the memory. To make this happen, an ART network has three layers: input (bottom), interface (middle), and category (top).

Figure 4.7 Stephen Grossberg pioneered psychophysical neural modeling.

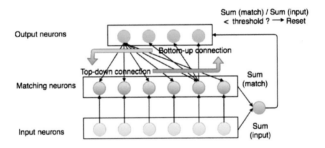

Figure 4.8 The ART1 network.

The input layer is set to input patterns and sends signals to the interface layer through one-to-one connections. The interface layer activates the category layer through full connections, and, in return, the category layer sends back activations to the interface layer through full connections. The interaction between the interface and category layer weights creates resonance. When an input pattern is presented to the input layer, the pattern is copied to the interface layer. Then, the category layer node whose input connection pattern is most similar to the input pattern wins and is activated. The winning category node sends back the top-down activation, which is a scaled version of the incoming connection pattern. Now, the interface layer receives two possibly different patterns; one is the input pattern, and the other is a feedback pattern, or top-down expectation, which is a pattern that reflects past learning. The interface layer nodes that receive inputs from both the input and the category layer nodes then become active. If there are enough active nodes in the interface layer compared to active nodes in the input layer, the category layer node is confirmed as the matching winner, and the top-down and bottom-up connections are updated to the scaled version of the pattern on the interface layer. If the match wasn't good enough, the category node is disabled temporarily, and the next-best matching category node is tested. If none of the existing category nodes match, then an unused category node is recruited, and the incoming connection pattern to the category node and the corresponding outgoing connection pattern are set to a scaled version of the input pattern. Other than ART1, many other neural network models accomplish grouping, such as learning vector quantization, invented by Teuvo Kohonen.

4.4 Unsupervised ANNs that compress

A cool trick for letting supervised ANNs do some unsupervised jobs is to give them only inputs; that is, teaching a supervised ANN to reproduce inputs. The task for the network is to output exactly the same pattern as the input; that way, we don't have a teaching signal. But what's the use of such a network? These networks usually have a middle layer that has a much smaller number of neurons, making an hourglass-like structure (Figure 4.9). After the network is trained to reproduce the inputs, it has learned to transform the input pattern to the middle layer pattern, which has a smaller number of elements and to reproduce the input on the output layer from the middle layer pattern. In other words, the network learns to encode a big input pattern to a small "code" that represents the input, which is why these networks are called *autoencoders*. The networks can also be used to remove noises (pixels affected by fluctuations in the light sensors for instance) because if we use an input slightly different from the learned one, an autoencoder tends to create the input that has already been learned instead of the minor variation. An autoencoder is also used to generate novel data by activating the middle layer.

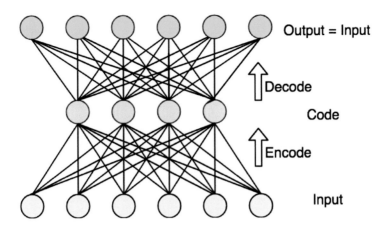

Figure 4.9 An autoencoder.

Questions

1. What is the data given during supervised learning but not in unsupervised learning?
2. In an SOFM, what happens to the map if one kind of input is given more frequently than others?
3. In an ART network, resonance is introduced to realize stable category formation. Resonance is established between the output layer and which layer?
4. What is formed at the middle layer of an autoencoder?

Answers

1. Desirable output (teacher signal); 2. The corresponding area becomes larger; 3. The interface (middle) layer; 4. The code.

5 ALGORITHMS THAT LEARN THROUGH TRIAL AND ERROR

5.1 Reinforcement learning: the third way

So far, you've learned about unsupervised learning and supervised learning, but sometimes these types of learning aren't applicable. For instance, suppose a baby is learning to walk. There is no way for the parents to tell the baby which muscles should be used in sequence, so supervised learning doesn't work. Observing sensory inputs or feedback from the feet and legs alone doesn't give the baby information about how to move them, so unsupervised learning doesn't work either. The best way for the baby to learn is to randomly generate movements and remember how they work in each situation. This type of learning is called reinforcement learning. *Reinforcement learning* is similar to supervised learning in that it receives an outside signal, but it's different because the signal isn't the correct output but an evaluation of how good the result of the action was. "Reinforcement" sounds like a big word, but it's closely related to how you learn things in daily life. In many cases, you try something and get rewarded when it goes well. Anything that increases the chance that you'll repeat the action you took is reinforcement. Hearing "Good job!" from your mom is one type of reinforcement, but getting a slice of pizza may be an even better form of reinforcement.

Reinforcement learning was originally a concept widely used in behavioral psychology. One of the pioneers in the development of reinforcement learning in the context of artificial intelligence (AI) is Richard Sutton, a Canadian computer scientist (Figure 5.1). In reinforcement learning, the learner (called the *agent*) produces an output (*action*) and then receives an evaluation signal (see the reinforcement learning concept in Figure 5.2). In addition to the *evaluation* signal, the agent also receives the new *state*. The state is the situation of the world observable or imaginable by the agent. The state changes as the agent creates an action, so the agent and the state form a loop. The evaluation signal is used to change the strategy for choosing the next action but isn't usually used to decide on the next action directly. Note that Figure 5.2 isn't a neural network diagram; the arrows aren't connections but they show the information flow.

Figure 5.1 Richard Sutton, one of the pioneers in reinforcement learning in artificial neural networks.

Action

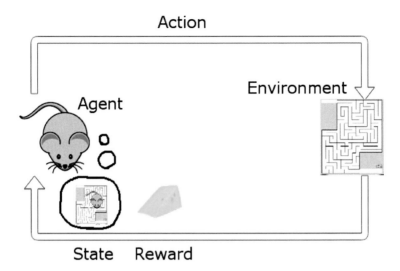

Environment

Agent

State   Reward

Figure 5.2 A schematic diagram showing the components of reinforcement learning.

Reinforcement learning is also good for training machines to play games, including video games and board games (Figure 5.3 and Figure 5.4). When playing games, the machine makes moves in the game and learns how much the situation improves or worsens. Examples of improved situations include more points in a video game, more opponent pieces in your hand in a board game, or eventually winning. Figure 5.3 shows a two-player table tennis video game developed by Atari, where one player is operated by the game machine. In this game screen, there are two paddles (green and orange rectangles), one black ball, and two black brackets. On the top are the scores of the two players. If you are the orange player, you can move the orange paddle to hit the ball. Your goal is to hit the ball so that the ball hits the bracket behind the green paddle without the green player being able to hit it back to you. The action is the movement of the orange paddle. The states are the position, speed, and direction of the ball. The reward is the game score.

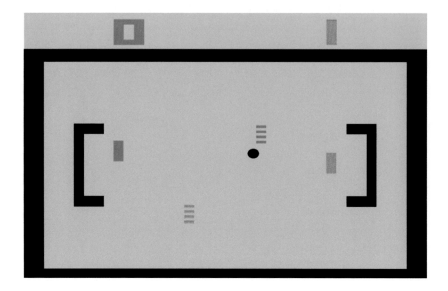

Figure 5.3 Reinforcement learning can be used to learn computer games effectively.

Another example is an AI system called AlphaGo, developed by Google's DeepMind team, that partly employed reinforcement learning and made history in 2016 when it beat Lee Sedol, an 18-time Go world champion (Figure 5.4. Google, DeepMind and AlphaGo are registered trademarks of Google Inc.).

As you can imagine, reinforcement learning works not only for babies and video games but also for certain kinds of robots for robot control—the robot chooses an action and receives the evaluation, which is used to improve the selection of the next actions (Figure 5.5). It's fun to watch robots learning to stand up and walk using reinforcement learning. Initially, the robot randomly shakes, stands up, and falls, but, after a while, the robot seems to find a strategy for moving in one direction. Sometimes, the robot finds a very creative solution, such as cartwheeling.

Figure 5.4 AI beats a Go champion.

Figure 5.5 A robot can learn to stand up and run.

5.2 Learning the situation (V-learning)

When you learn something, such as learning to perform martial arts or to maneuver a boat on a river, it's also important to learn how good or bad your situation is. How good is it if you take your opponent's leg? How bad is it if the boat just seems to be rotating when you are rowing? Value learning (V-learning) does just that: it places a value on the situation.

In V-learning, the system learns to determine how good or bad a situation is. Let's say the situation is **s**, which can be anything that represents a situation. For instance, we can assign numbers to situations, such as situation 1, situation 2, and so on, or situations can be represented by thousands of numbers if the situation is made of many elements, such as dots in a video game. If the number of situations is not too big, you can use a lookup dictionary to look under **s** and find the value V. If we consider the current reward as the only indicator of the value in the current situation, the learning is very simple. That is, if, after some action, the situation changes to **s**, and the evaluation of this new situation is **r**, you can write **r** to a list entry at **s** (Figure 5.6).

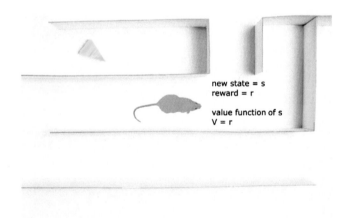

state	...	**s**	...
value	...	**r**	...

Figure 5.6 Simple V-learning after reaching state **s**.

Unfortunately, **r** is not always consistent, as there can be random fluctuations, or the evaluation may depend on other unknown factors. In that case, we can pull V to **r** a little each time so that V approaches its average value. The difference between the old value of V (*V_old*) and **r** is *r − V_old*, so if we add this difference to *V_old*, it immediately becomes the new **r**. Instead, we can change the V a little each time by adding a fraction of *r − V_old*, for instance, *0.1 * (r − V_old)* (Figure 5.7).

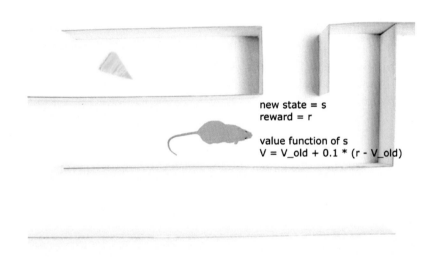

state	...	s	...
value	...	**V_old +** **0.1 * (r − V_old)**	...

Figure 5.7 V-learning with smoothing after reaching state **s**.

But where is the neural network? If we're just updating a lookup table, this isn't a neural network. When there are only a few states, there is no need to use neural networks. Instead, we only need a table that stores the average evaluation for each state (or action-state pair). However, this quickly becomes impractical when there are a large number of states, as in a case where the state is defined by all the voxels in the game display. This is where the neural network comes in. Because we can no longer keep V for all possible instances of **s**, we train a neural network to output *r* when the input is **s**, allowing the use of supervised learning.

So far, though, the current situation **s** only takes credit for the current evaluation **r**, which often isn't enough, as the effect of the action taken may influence the improvement of the situation in the future. Additionally, some systems may not provide a reward until the agent clearly wins. So, let's consider the effect of the current action on the goodness of the situation after the current action (Figure 5.8). With the degree of the effect **g** of the future situation (**g** is greater than 0 and less than 1; below, we assume 0.5), we will use a modified evaluation *r + 0.5 * V_next* instead of **r**, where *V_next* is the evaluation of the best possible next situation (**s'** in Figure 5.8). Note that *V_next* is looked up from the current table, before any update. With this change, the table update will be as shown in Figure 5.8. Adding a fraction of future gain is called *temporal difference reinforcement learning* and is credited to Richard Sutton mentioned previously (Sutton 1988)[8]. If the table becomes too big, we can again use a neural network to output *r + g * V_next* when the inputs are **s** and **a**.

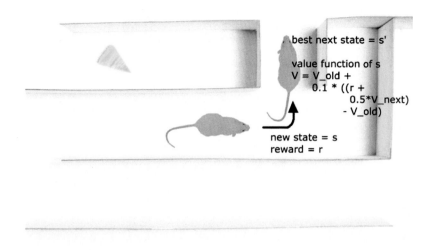

best next state = s'

value function of s
V = V_old +
0.1 * ((r +
0.5*V_next)
- V_old)

new state = s
reward = r

state	...	s	...
value	...	V_old + 0.1 * ((r+0.5*V_next) − V_old)	...

Figure **5.8** Temporal difference V-learning with smoothing after reaching state **s**, after which the mouse can reach state **s'**.

A classic example of V-learning is neural pole balancing demonstrated on a computer (Figure 5.9). Suppose you hold a long stick on your palm, and you must move your hand horizontally, so the stick doesn't fall. In this case, the states are the position and the speed of your arm, the action is the movement of your palm, and you get rewards when the pole is closer to upright. Using neural networks makes sense here because the number of states is infinite.

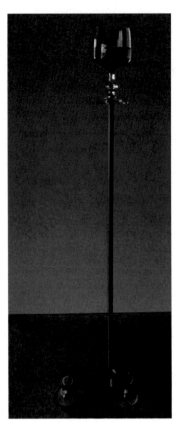

Figure 5.9 Reinforcement learning can be used to balance a pole.

5.3 Learning to act in the situation (Q-learning)

Instead of learning how good each situation s is, we can be a little more ambitious and learn how good it is to take a specific action **a** in the situation **s**. For instance, let's say **s** is the arrangement of pieces on a chessboard, and **a** is one of the possible moves. As in V-learning, we can start by taking action **a** in situation **s** and writing the resultant evaluation **r** in a lookup table—this time a table with rows and columns, instead of a list (Figure 5.10).

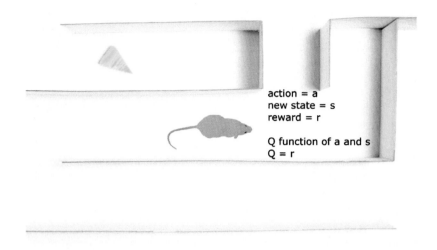

action = a
new state = s
reward = r

Q function of a and s
Q = r

action\state	...	s	...
:			
a	...	r	...
:			

Figure 5.10 Simple Q-learning after taking action **a** and reaching state **s**.

After the table is filled in, you can use it to locate the best action by looking through the entries with the current situation **s**. As in V-learning, you can smooth out different evaluations of the same situation-action pair by moving the table entries a little each time as $Q\_old + 0.1 * (r - Q\_old)$ (Figure 5.11).

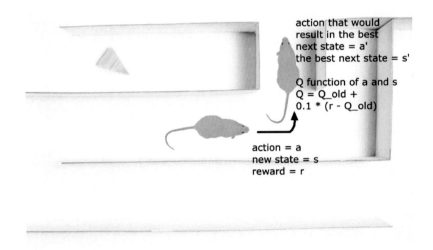

action that would
result in the best
next state = a'
the best next state = s'

Q function of a and s
Q = Q_old +
0.1 * (r - Q_old)

action = a
new state = s
reward = r

action\state	...	s	...
:			
a	...	**Q_old +** **0.1 * (r − Q_old)**	...
:			

Figure 5.11 Q-learning with smoothing after taking action **a** and reaching state **s**.

Again, as in V-learning, you can extend Q-learning to consider the effect of the current action on the goodness of the situation after the next action. With the degree of the effect **g** (again, we assume 0.5), we can use the modified reward $r + 0.5 * Q\_next$, where Q_next is the table entry for the best-possible next situation **s'** and the action **a'** that will bring about that state. Remember that Q_next is looked up on the current table, before any update. Lastly, instead of using a lookup table, you can train a neural network using supervised learning to output **r** or $r + g * Q\_next$ when the input is **s** and **a** (Figure 5.12). Temporal difference Q-learning can be used to train a program to play video games.

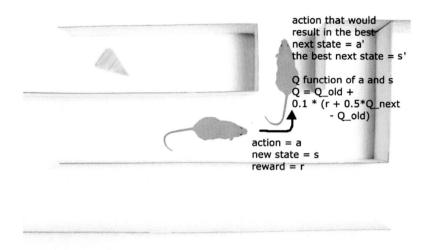

action that would
result in the best
next state = a'
the best next state = s'

Q function of a and s
Q = Q_old +
0.1 * (r + 0.5*Q_next
        - Q_old)

action = a
new state = s
reward = r

action\state	...	s	...
:			
a	...	Q_old + 0.1 * (r + 0.5 * Q_next − Q_old)	...
:			

Figure 5.12 Temporal difference Q-learning with smoothing after taking action **a** and reaching state **s**, after which the mouse can take action **a** to reach state **s**.

5.4 Autonomous cars

Along with robotics and game playing, reinforcement learning is also applied to autonomous, or self-driving, cars. Using reinforcement learning, the program learns to assess driving situations using cameras and other sensors before generating actions (accelerate, apply the brake, turn the wheel, etc.). Unlike robot training, we can't afford to let the program generate actions randomly on the real road, causing accidents, so the program is trained using recorded scenes and simulators. Autonomous cars have come a long way, and it's amazing to see them maneuvering in tricky situations. However, the technology is still in development. It takes a huge amount of data, realistic simulators, and a lengthy training time for the program to learn, and, after all that, the program still tends to have problems, especially when dealing with cars driven by humans. The program must also learn not to confuse human drivers by making non-humanlike maneuvers, even if the evaluation function of the road says they are perfect.

Figure 5.13 A self-driving car tested in Brazil.

Questions

1. Does reinforcement learning get inputs and produce outputs too?
2. In reinforcement learning, what kind of response does the agent get from its environment?
3. Both V-learning and Q-learning determine how good the new state is, but Q-learning learns the evaluation specific to something in addition to the state. What is it?
4. What can reinforcement learning use when an ANN is not required because of the limited number of states and actions?

Answers
Yes; 2. New state and reward; 3. Action; 4. A table.

6 TALKING ARTIFICIAL NEURAL NETWORKS

6.1 How does a voice-controlled personal assistant work?

You say, "How about some music?" to your voice-controlled personal assistant, and it starts playing your favorite artists. Or, you can ask for a joke, and it seems to know what you're talking about, at least in many cases (Figure 6.1).

Figure 6.1 A voice-controlled personal assistant.

As you can imagine, AI is behind those responses, tackling the very difficult tasks of understanding your speech when there's a lot of unrelated background noise, judging how to respond to you in real time properly, and acting or answering using a natural-sounding voice. An ANN is also involved but not as the sole component. Behind a voice-controlled personal assistant is a complex system composed of voice recognition, linguistic analysis, conversational control, database and web content retrieval, and voice systems, to name a few, and all of these components must cooperate to respond to you in under a few seconds to carry on natural conversations. The boundaries between these components aren't as rigid as they once were because ANNs have begun to replace big chunks of the system, but it's also not as easy as hooking up a microphone and a speaker to a gigantic ANN.

6.2 Speech recognition

When creating a voice-controlled personal assistant, you first need a system to recognize your speech. Engineers have struggled with this for decades. If you get a 95 score out of 100 on a test, you did great. But if a speech recognition system recognizes 95% of your words, it's really annoying because if the system mistakes one out of 20 words $((20 - 1)/20 = 0.95)$, that could be one word in each written sentence. Andrew Ng, a researcher in AI and ANNs, predicted that if the speech recognition rate improves from 95% to 99%, speech input will become the primary mode of communicating with computers. In recent years, ANNs have contributed quite a lot to bringing this prediction closer to reality. A speech-recognition system does what our ears do: converts speech sounds—a continuous change in air pressure—into a continuous change in frequencies. Here, we aren't talking about a melody that has one frequency each time but rather about harmonies—a mixture of frequencies (called a spectrum) at each point, as shown in Figure 6.2. This can be fed to an ANN, which translates these frequencies into a series of linguistic sounds, such as /h/ /e/ /e/ /e/ /i/ (for "Hey" with a long "eh" in the middle). This series of sounds then can be converted into words and phrases.

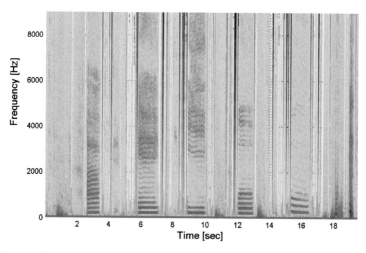

Figure 6.2 Spectrogram of some vowels (German vowels "a, e, i, o, u").

6.3 Sequence processing

Here, we focus on a system that processes language; this is used after a voice-recognition system that converts a stream of speech sounds into words. How should the words be represented in an ANN? This may sound like a stupid question. After all, why not just type the words into a computer as a string of the alphabet for input? As it turns out, representing a word by the characters in the word is *not* so helpful. For one thing, we must use different number of letters to represent different words, which is inconvenient for computers. Plus, there is no hint in the word "c-a-t" that it's an animal like a dog, which meows instead of barks. The simplest way is to assign different neurons to different words. This is the easiest and the cleanest in some sense because all words are treated equally, but the representation of each word does not reflect any meanings. To add more information, it's common to represent a word with a group of words the original word is often used with.

Suppose neurons are assigned to different words, as already suggested. You can go through a huge number of books or blog posts to find out how often the word appears after which words, and how often the word in question appears before which words. Take five words: {Cats, Dogs, bark, meow, eat}. By assigning one neuron to each, the representations for Cats, Dogs, bark, meow, and eat are {(1,0,0,0,0), (0,1,0,0,0), (0,0,1,0,0), (0,0,0,1,0), and (0,0,0,0,1)}. If you have only four sentences—"Cats meow," "Dogs bark," "Cats eat," and "Dogs eat" (Figure 6.3)—"Cats" appears before "meow" and "eat," which can be expressed as (0,0,0,1,1). "Cats" doesn't appear after any words, which can be expressed as (0,0,0,0,0). In this case, "Cats" is represented as (0,0,0,0,0, 0,0,0,1,1). This method of representing words can be extended to include relationships between distant words (not just next words). Another method is to take neighboring words in a wider scope without considering the exact word order; this is called the bag-of-words model. Representation of words in these ways are called *word embeddings*.

Now that we've settled on the representation of words, let's tackle the next difficulty when processing language: time. "I am hungry," is different from, "Am I hungry" because the word order is different. So, when an ANN works on a sentence, it needs to remember what it has previously processed before it hears the next word. This is usually done by having a neuron group that "remembers" what has been heard and uses that memory as an input to the network along with the next word. When the network receives "am" in "I am hungry," it also receives signals from a neuron group that remembers "I." When the network receives "hungry," it also receives signals from a neuron group that represents "I am." In the end, the neuron group represents, "I am hungry." One example of this type of network is shown in Figure 6.4. The network remembers the word it has seen by sending the hidden layer activation back to the right input. This type of ANN is called a recurrent neural network (RNN) because it has a loop in the connection to feed the previous activations back to the input (Figure 6.2). This network receives one word at a time and is trained to generate an output each time using supervised learning. Interestingly, you can train a recurrent network to predict the next word. This way, the network can be trained using supervised learning without needing to generate additional "desired outputs". The network acquires some aspect of the grammar because it's needed to predict the next word. RNNs are also powerful because they can be trained to represent not just words but also phrases and sentences in a group of neurons.

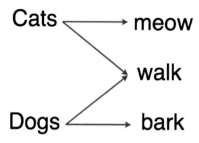

Figure 6.3 Word order in a miniature grammar.

Training an RNN can be done using supervised learning, and, more specifically, by using the backpropagation that was introduced in Chapters 2 and 3. However, this process is more complicated than training an ANN with no loops. Remember, in backpropagation an error is computed for the intermediate layers by transmitting errors from the output toward the input. Because RNN has loops, the error also flows from the input toward the output direction. To solve this, there is a process that removes loops called *unfolding*. To show this process, we simplify the diagram in Figure 6.4 by representing connections from a layer of neurons to another layer of neurons by a single arrow, as in the left network in Figure 6.5. The loops are removed by duplicating parts of the neural network whenever they represent different parts of the sentence (Figure 6.5, right). After unfolding, we can train the RNN the way we train ANNs without loops; as more words are fed into the network, the words are processed as if the past words are present and fed through a repeated version of the hidden layers. We assume that the repeated layers share the same set of connection weights.

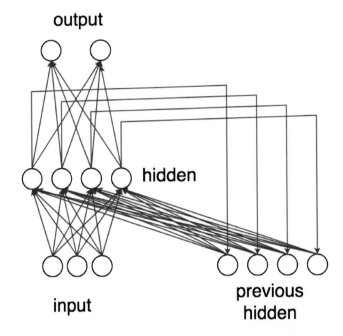

Figure 6.4 A recurrent neural network.

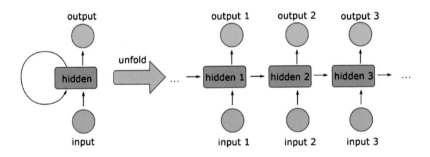

Figure 6.5 A schematic representation of a recurrent artificial neural network and its unfolding to remove loops.

One type of RNN model that you must know about if you're interested in these talking neural networks has a very indecisive-sounding name: the long short-term memory (LSTM) model. Humans are thought to have two kinds of memory: long-term memory and short-term memory. Short-term memories are things you rehearse in your mind and keep for a short period, such as memorizing a phone number to make a phone call. After you've made the call, you often no longer remember the number. Long-term memory, on the other hand, is something you remember for days, months, or years, such as your friend's name. In neural networks, memories stored related to the connection strength between neurons are called long-term memories, and memories stored related to the activity pattern of the neurons are called short-term memories. The LSTM does have long-term memory and short-term memory components. However, unlike short-term memory in a standard recurrent neural network, which changes every time a new input is presented, the short-term memory in the LSTM can be kept unchanged as several inputs are processed. Without going into too much detail, the structure of a typical LSTM is shown in Figure 6.6. The trick is that the LSTM has a short-term memory that can be kept or rewritten, depending on the current short-term memory, input, and connection weights. Compared to a simple RNN, where the memory naturally decays over time, LSTM can control how long it holds the current memory. This makes LSTM a powerful tool for natural language processing.

A special kind of RNN can be constructed to encode a sequence of inputs to an activation pattern in a neural layer and to another sequence from the activity pattern (Figure 6.7). You can think of this network as encoding a sequence of words into an activity pattern that represents the sentence and decoding this pattern into another sequence. You can use this type of neural network to translate an English sentence into a Spanish one. The English and Spanish sentences don't have to be of the same length because the decoding can stop at the period in English, and the Spanish sentence can be generated until it generates a period in Spanish. The pattern of activation after the RNN reads an English sentence can be said to represent the sentence (the fourth rectangle from the left in Figure 6.7). If the translation requires a lot of thinking about the sentence's meaning, not just a word-by-word translation, the representation of a sentence can be thought of as some aspect of the "meaning" of the sentence, which is related to "thought vector," a phrase popularized Geoffrey Hinton, one of the founders of artificial neural network research. There is a danger in oversimplifying "thought" in this way, but it's intriguing that thoughts could be translated into a series of numbers (a vector).

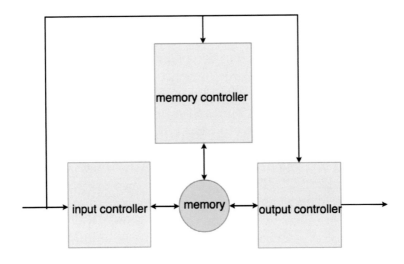

Figure 6.6 The structure of a long short-term memory.

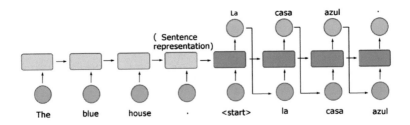

Figure 6.7 Sequence-to-sequence (English to Spanish) conversion via a sentence representation.

6.4 Task execution

With a virtual assistant, the task of the center unit (between speech recognition and production) is to translate the voice input into commands that the assistant can execute, such as turning on a light, showing web search results, or translating one language into another. If the command is more complicated than the small assistant device can handle, it sends a request through the Internet to a bigger computer system (server) for processing. This is a daunting task for a machine because the scope of the things people say is huge and unpredictable. Someone might say, "How much does a T-Rex weigh?" or, "Uh, . . . I'm bored." Sometimes the speech is not clear, or the speech is clear, but the meaning isn't; in these cases, the assistant may have to ask probing questions.

The final stage of a voice-controlled personal assistant is speech synthesis. This is technically easier to do than speech recognition if the goal is to create speech sounds that humans can understand because humans are so good at understanding speech. Speech synthesis is accomplished using an RNN that converts a series of linguistic sounds into a series of spectrum (Figure 6.2). However, the kind of naturalistic speech where you can't tell if it was created by man or machine hasn't been accomplished yet. It's difficult to generate speech that has not only correct sounds but also has natural sounds when combined in a long sequence, with natural pitch changes over time, and the ability to convey natural emotions.

In this chapter, we've looked at a voice-controlled personal assistant, which is just one example of an AI-powered natural language processing application. A chatbot is another interesting type of application that shows how AI-based natural language processing can be used (Figure 6.8). Currently, chatbots are used for entertainment, customer support, online shopping, education, travel, and so on—the list is endless.

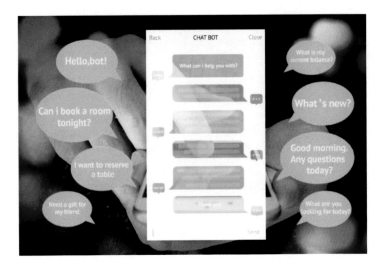

Figure 6.8 Conversation with a chatbot on the phone.

Questions

1. What are the first and last main components of a virtual assistant?
2. What does an RNN have that a simple three-layer neural network doesn't have?
3. What does LSTM stand for?
4. Compared to regular RNN, LSTM has better control over keeping or updating the state of one component. What is it?

Answers

1. Speech recognition and speech generation; 2. A loop; 3. Long short-term memory; 4. The short-term memory.

7 ARTIFICIAL NEURAL NETWORKS AND BIOLOGICAL NEURAL NETWORKS

7.1 Why study the brain?

ANNs were originally inspired by the human brain. The basic artificial neuron that multiplies the inputs with the connection weights, accumulates the results, and applies output function is certainly a model of a biological neuron at an abstract level. In the 1970s, researchers performed a lot of cognitive neural modeling in an attempt to emulate and study the cognitive functions of the brain. Recently, especially after "deep learning" neural networks were successfully applied to many engineering problems, there hasn't been a lot of interaction between ANN researchers and neuroscientists. Even at a single neuron level, the similarity between a biological neuron and an artificial neuron breaks down easily if we look at the process more closely because a real neuron is made of tiny electrochemical processes that are only roughly approximated in an artificial neuron model. In addition, it is unlikely that backpropagation, one of the most powerful algorithms for training ANNs, is going on in the brain when people learn, although some researchers are trying to see if some neural mechanisms can be interpreted as implementing backpropagation.

It can be argued that it is not necessary for AI to imitate the way the brain works. As an analogy, airplanes fly much faster with jet engines fixed to their wings than by flapping wings as birds do. So, it may be okay that learning by backpropagation is very different from the way the human brain learns. In fact, AI is starting to beat human performance in many areas (computing, playing games, etc.), which may lead some people to believe there's not much AI researchers can learn from the brain.

However, there are two reasons we should watch for developments in neuroscience. First, there are still areas where people perform much better than AI. Second, it appears that the ANNs and biological neural networks operate in very different ways, indicating that the current ANN may not be operating as nature developed, so there may be a totally different operating principle we can learn from. Let's examine these two points in turn.

7.2 Areas where artificial neural networks may be able to learn from human performance

In some ways, the human brain works much better than ANNs do. For instance, we just saw that recent progress in AI has a lot to do with the huge amounts of data that are available for training neural networks. It's nice that ANNs can learn, but it looks like, in some cases, children can learn much faster from only a few examples. Even when trained on a limited number of samples, people seem to make fewer hilarious mistakes than ANNs. This motivated the development of new kinds of fast-learning algorithms. One model is the *graphical model*, which has nodes and arrows (or lines), as shown in Figure 7.1. The nodes describe anything that can be represented by numbers or labels, and the arrows and lines show how likely one node's value ends up with the given value of another node. Five variables are represented in Figure 7.1: the difficulty of the courses, students' intelligence, students' course grades, students' SAT scores, and the favorability of the recommendation letters the students' receive from the course teachers. The difficulty of the course and the intelligence of the student affect the student's grade. The SAT score is influenced by the student's intelligence but has nothing to do with the classes. The grade affects whether the student gets a good recommendation letter. Graphical models can be trained faster than commonly used ANN models.

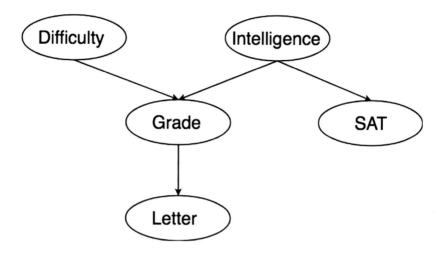

Figure 7.1 A graphical model representing the probabilistic relationships between five variables: the difficulty of courses, students' intelligence, students' course grades, students' SAT scores, and the favorability of the recommendation letters the students' receive from the course teachers.

Another thing that humans have but machines seem to lack is creativity. However, ANN models called the *generative model* can create examples after learning (see Box 3.1 for an example image created by a generative model). One of the most popular generative models, called a generative adversarial network (GAN), learns to generate outputs indistinguishable from the real data (Figure 7.2).

Humans also seem to have the ability to transfer learning to new areas. For instance, after learning how to draw cats, it may be easier to learn how to draw dogs than it would have been learning how to draw them from scratch. Similarly, a network trained in one game may be able to be trained for a new game faster than being trained from scratch. Similarly, a robot that learned to use its arm in one situation may be able to learn to use the arm in a totally new situation much faster. Transfer learning works better if the original task and the applied task have some common features. For instance, an image-processing network may develop feature detectors at the layers close to the input image that correspond to dots, lines, and so on, which can be used in many different image-processing programs. However, keep in mind that transfer learning in ANNs doesn't always come without a price. If one network is too specialized in one task, it may be difficult for that network to learn other tasks. Transfer learning in ANNs requires some consideration regarding the structure and training schedule to make transfer learning easier.

Another thing humans often do when planning a task is an imaginary rehearsal. You can play out in your imagination how you would move a piece in chess and see whether that might go well before carrying it out. It has been observed that a "replay" of a sequence of neural events appears in a part of the brain called the hippocampus (we'll talk about this weird-sounding name and what it means later, in Box 7.1). Researchers are experimenting with neural networks that can imagine things—for instance, the generative models mentioned earlier—to mimic mental rehearsals.

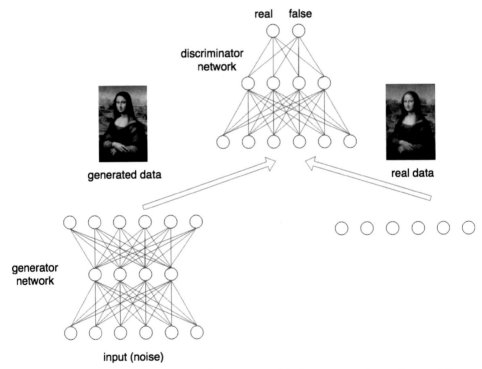

Figure 7.2 A schematic diagram explaining generative adversarial networks, a popular ANN model.

At a very fundamental level, humans develop an intuitive understanding of the physical world, such as space and number, at a very early age. You rarely notice this consciously because it's so ingrained in your mind, but it's a hard task to acquire the fundamental notions of space, number, and quantity, and practically apply these notions to an artificial network.

7.3 Biological neural networks

In 7.2 we discussed the possible contribution of neuroscience at a functional level in cognitive neuroscience and functional brain-imaging studies. But there is also a different line of neuroscience called *computational neuroscience* that might contribute to new developments in ANNs. Instead of trying to find out how the brain functions at a cognitive level, computational neuroscience examines how the small components of neurons and synapses work, and then analyzes in detail the raw signals the neurons and groups of neurons create. Computational neuroscientists record from a single cell or put sensors in the brains of mice and record from many cells as the animals run in a maze to find cheese. It's not an easy task to record or understand the signals, so researchers around the world are also running computer simulations of minute processes within a neuron and building up the neuron and neural cell assemblies in the computer to try to replicate the signals observed from cells and cell assemblies (Figure 7.5). Together, they are attempting to uncover the design of neurons and the nervous system.

At the cell level, neurons aren't just the simple calculators that multiply and add, as was once assumed. Instead, smaller processes involving molecules carry electric charges. When a signal reaches a neuron, the neuron opens or closes tiny gates that control the flow of charged particles that go inside or outside the neuron, changing the voltage of parts of the neuron. This creates current flow around the gates and causes voltage changes. Depending on the geometry of the cell (Figure 7.3), a single cell may perform a very complex operation that isn't considered in simple neuron models. For instance, the positions of the synapses, and the merging order of the dendrites may affect the effect of the connections through the synapses.

Even the basic distinctions, such as connections and activities, are simplified notions because there are fast-changing connections that change more slowly than the electrical activities, but still occur many times per second. These quick connection weight changes may change the grouping of the cells that work together, which makes complex temporal processing possible.

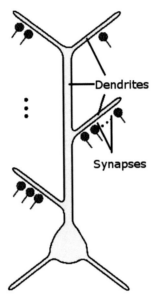

Figure 7.3 A neuron can compute more than just one big sum of weighted inputs.

At a neural-assembly level, the "big brain" of humans is made of six layers organized into columns, which is a remarkably regular structure for the brain's complex functioning (Figure 7.4). Although we know there are many types of neurons, and we have some knowledge about how these cell types are distributed in the layers and columns, we don't precisely understand how the layers and columns work. Once we find out, our understanding of the brain may change, which may impact ANN technology.

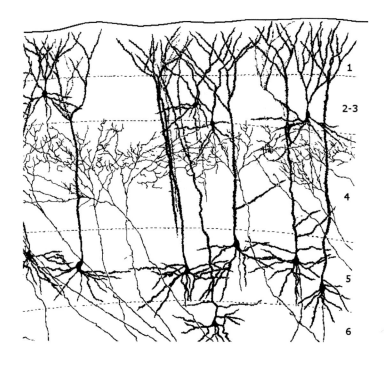

Figure 7.4 A common structure of the surface of the human brain. The numbers 1 to 6 indicate layer numbers from the surface of the cortex.

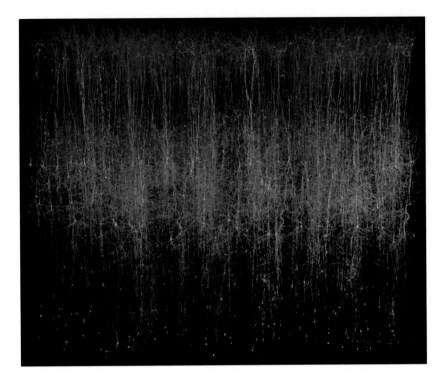

Figure 7.5 A computer simulation of the activities of a small circuit in the rat brain. The simulation was conducted as a part of Human Brain Project funded by the European Union.

Humans and many animals have rhythmic electrical activities in the brain called brainwaves (Figure 7.6). Human brainwaves were first recorded by German psychiatrist Hans Berger in 1924. The most famous brainwave is the alpha wave, which appears when you close your eyes and relax. Big brainwaves, such as alpha waves, can be recorded using an EEG, which involves putting electrodes on the skin of the head and recording voltages. Some researchers in neuroscience think brainwaves are an important part of information processing in the brain. For instance, when a mouse runs in a familiar landscape, the strength and timing of a brainwave called the theta wave encodes the mouse's position and speed. Interestingly, we can predict what the mouse will do by recording the brainwaves before the mouse takes the definitive action. Most ANN models don't generate brainwaves, which is an indication that the real brain has some different operating principles.

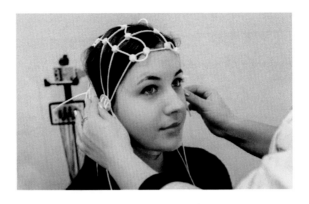

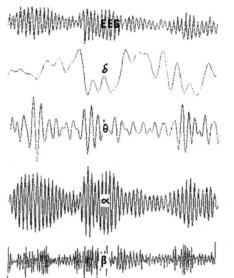

Figure 7.6 An EEG equipment and brain rhythms. Top: setting up electrodes of a brainwave recorder (EEG). Bottom: Brainwaves, from top: the whole EEG wave, the delta wave component, the theta wave component, the alpha wave component, the beta wave component.

In essence, we don't really know how the brain works, but neuroscientists are working hard to find out. It may take a long time before this research will be relevant to ANNs. It's up to future AI researchers and developers, which some of you will become, to decide whether ANNs can incorporate some of the findings and ideas from neuroscience.

7.4 The brain–machine interface

One interesting area for both neuroscientists and engineers is the brain–machine interface (Figure 7.7). Research has shown that we can determine what a person has decided in his or her mind by reading brain images. We can also predict an animal's motion by reading the electrical activities from electrodes implanted in the animal's head. So, although we still don't know the details about how the decision is represented in the brain, we do know how to recognize the decision from measured activities, and how to use that knowledge to control machines. This knowledge can be used for developing brain-controlled devices for people with disabilities. For instance, people who can't move their hands can be trained to "type" by thinking the letters.

Figure 7.7 Controlling a model car with the brain.

The brain–machine interface can also work in the opposite direction—from machines to neurons. For instance, people who can't hear because they have damaged hearing organs can sense sounds by connecting a sound analyzer to sensory neurons. Or people who are blind can sense brightness and shapes by connecting light sensors to sensory neurons. Besides being useful, research in neural human–machine interfaces may someday advance our understanding of how information is represented in the human brain. Eventually, the brain–machine interface may lead to the development of androids, which are humans augmented by machines, or machines augmented by living cells.

Box 7.1 Hippocampus

The hippocampus is a curious part of the brain. It has a strange name and odd shape, and, above all, it fascinates brain researchers by its enigmatic functions (Figure 7.8). First, we must talk about its name. Why does it sound like hippopotamus? Hippocampus and hippopotamus share "hippo," which comes from a Greek word that means "horse." "Campus" in hippocampus comes from "sea dragon" in Greek. Apparently, someone thought this part of the brain looked like a seahorse. By the way, "potamus" in hippopotamus means "river" in ancient Greek, so someone must have thought that a hippopotamus looked like a horse in the river. Maybe horses in those days were chubbier than modern horses. Hippocampus is an old part of the brain in terms of evolution, separate from the new brain, such as the cerebrum (the big brain). Mammals, including humans, have two hippocampi.

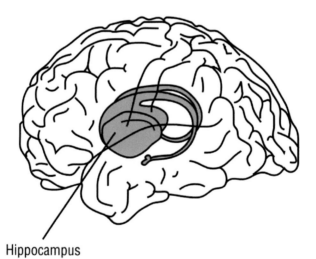

Hippocampus

Figure 7.8 Human Hippocampus

The human hippocampus plays an important role in short-term memory and memory consolidation (transfer of short-term memory to long-term memory). In fact, long-term changes in connections among neurons were first discovered in the hippocampus. Elderly people who have memory problems often have problems in the hippocampus. As an example, a famous epilepsy patient Henry Gustav Molaison (1926-2008) widely known by his initials H. M. had parts of his hippocampus removed in an attempt to relieve his epilepsy symptoms. As a side effect of the surgery, he had a memory consolidation problem and lost the ability to form new memories. For instance, he remembered the faces of famous people he knew before the surgery, but he couldn't remember new faces.

In rodents, the hippocampus is associated with spatial memory and navigation. Many cells in a rodent's hippocampus are "place cells" that fire when the animal is at a particular position in its surroundings (Figure 7.9 right).

Figure 7.9 Researchers who investigated navigation-related cells. Left: researchers awarded Nobel Prizes for physiology and medicine for their research in the hippocampus and surrounding cortex in rodents (from left, Edvard Mozer, May-Britt Mozer, John O'Keefe). Right: eight different place cells in a rodent responded to eight different sections in the maze.

Questions

1. What is the part of the brain that has to do with an animal walking in a maze?
2. How many layers does the cortex of the human big brain have?
3. What is the name of the neural network that can generate examples of what it has learned but has not yet seen?
4. What is the name of the neural network that uses nodes to represent numbers/labels and lines to represent the statistical relationships among them?

Answers

1. Hippocampus; 2. Six; 3. Generative model; 4. Graphical model.

8 ARTIFICIAL INTELLIGENCE: TODAY AND TOMORROW

8.1 Cutting edge

AI is being used more and more, and you'll likely see its use increase in the near future. As you've learned, AI is used in voice-controlled personal assistants, self-driving cars, and medical diagnoses—and the list continues to grow. All sorts of smart machines and services will be available that we might not even think are particularly AI-powered. Using these devices and services will make our lives easier and more convenient. On the other hand, issues may arise in delegating human thinking to machines and letting the machines work independently of humans.

Let's start with the bright side. What amazing things can we do with AI? A significant application of AI is in medicine; for example, in finding new drugs (Figure 8.1). Drug discovery costs companies billions of dollars and years of development and testing. With the vast knowledge of patients, patents, chemical structures, and genomics stored in databases, AI systems can search for potentially effective treatments more quickly and with higher accuracy than human experts can. AI is also used for medical diagnoses and for finding treatments that best match individual patients.

Figure 8.1 AI-assisted drug discovery. Combining chemical structure analysis and the analysis of the biological activity of chemicals, AI can accelerate drug discovery.

Natural language applications, such as machine translation and natural language interfaces, have shown impressive progress. AI-powered natural language processing is also used behind the scenes as AI systems extract knowledge from natural language texts. The knowledge here doesn't just refer to logical meanings in the traditional sense that can be used in debate (see what Aristotle says in Figure 1.5). Neural networks are also used to classify the topics of texts, detect the sentiments (likes or dislikes) texts convey, and judge how readable the texts are.

Some applications of AI are aimed at taking care of us. Robots that take care of patients in general, and the elderly specifically, are in development (Figure 8.2). People are surprisingly open to interacting with robots after they find that robots behave in a friendly way.

How about a robot as a friend? Some robots even have emotional capabilities. A Japanese robot released in 2015 (Figure 8.3) "reads" your emotions and then tries to make you feel better. It also becomes better friends with you over time by learning. But who will take care of the robots? Don't worry, researchers are also developing robots that diagnose and repair themselves.

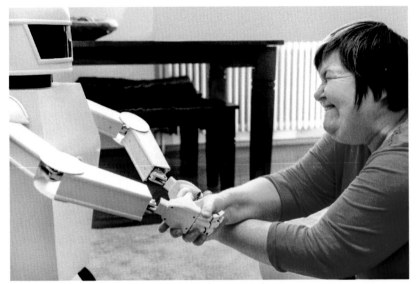

Figure 8.2 A care robot.

Figure 8.3 A robot that analyzes and responds to emotion.

Robots can also be used in dangerous situations or situations we want to avoid, such as in old minefields, automobile factories, on other planets, and places with ultra-high or ultra-low temperatures (Figure 8.4). Machines have already been used in such environments, but AI can make the machines more autonomous and useful. For instance, you can't control a robot on Mars from Earth because it takes 4 to 24 minutes, depending on where the two planets are, for radio waves to travel.

Figure 8.4 Robots can work in hazardous environments.

Finance is another area where AI has been used. It is difficult to predict whether the stock price of companies will go up or down, and by how much. This problem, called stock prediction, has always been a battleground for different methods, including mathematics, computer algorithms, and AI. AI promises to combine mathematical analysis, news analysis, and emotional analysis of the market to provide an accurate prediction of stock prices.

Some AI-related news should be read with caution because a fair amount of hype is often involved, or a special condition in which the intelligence is demonstrated is ignored in the reports. For instance, recently a test of the conversational skill of AI—called the Turing Test—was reportedly passed by a program named Eugene Goostman, but the program portrayed itself as a 13-year-old Ukrainian boy, which was intended to cause judges to forgive grammatical errors or lack of certain knowledge. In a competition, the program convinced 33% of the judges they were conversing with a real human being through typing, exceeding the 30% required by the Turing Test. Though this is impressive, in some ways it hasn't fully passed the original intent of the test, because the program won by lowering the expectations of the judges.

Keep in mind that real-world applications (not toy programs) using AI have just begun, and AI technology hasn't fully matured and been tested. One way you can easily see that AI isn't up to its mark is to try language translation on a web browser. Sometimes, the translation is so poor you can't understand what it really means.

8.2 Future

In the far future, we expect AI to be more integrated with us, literally. Our brains will be able to communicate with AI more directly—through implanted electrodes, for instance. AI will be used to interface our brain and machines to expand our cognitive capabilities. Unfortunately, development in this direction may take many years because we must do more research on the human brain side, as described in the previous chapter. But, like all other fields in science, we're making progress. The neural representation problem might look like an impossible problem right now, but it will be solved—the only question is when.

AI might have bigger tasks on its shoulders. Some researchers think AI can solve some of the gravest human problems, such as poverty, hunger, and climate change. Global problems require fast global data acquisition, statistical analysis, knowledge, and strategic thinking, which AI will continue to improve upon. Maybe there will be a global think tank in the future that will be run by a collaboration of big AI programs.

All the future developments of AI will be reinforced by developments in the supporting hardware. In Chapter 2, we mentioned the progress in memory, processors, and special integrated circuits called GPUs. New computer designs are on the horizon. One design represents the activity of the neurons in a manner closer to biological neurons. A biological neuron integrates the inputs and decides whether it generates a spike (positive output, in Figure 2.1) or not (zero output). At a given time, a neuron is either spiking or not spiking. However, most conventional neural network models use continuous values representing the spiking frequencies of neurons. Spiking neural networks consider the spike timings rather than just the spiking frequency, which seems to be an important feature of biological neural networks. Spiking neural networks can be simulated by traditional computers, but implementing them in special hardware saves energy consumption.

Another computer design on the horizon is the quantum computer (Figure 8.5). Quantum computers, once fully developed, will be faster and smaller than conventional computers because they operate on numbers that behave rather mysteriously — each number in a quantum computer can have different values at once with different probabilities. These numbers are realized in quantum devices with a super cool (literally: at nearly -460 Fahrenheit or -273 Centigrade) and super small elements, where quantum physics is required to describe the behavior of the materials.

Figure 8.5 Research on quantum computing is accelerating.

You will also hear about a class of AI called artificial general intelligence (AGI). In most AI applications, AI is developed and applied to solve specific problems; for instance, drug discovery, machine translation, or image processing. AGI is a more generic, human-like intelligence that can tackle problems by developing and applying general cognitive abilities across different areas. Many people are skeptical of AGI, however. For instance, Peter Bentley, a computer scientist, and Steven Pinker, a cognitive scientist, think that the progress in AI will be made only by tackling specific problems that must be solved, not by trying to advance machine intelligence in general. In other words, intelligence is not one single ability that improves over time. In this view, it's wrong to think that the progress of AI can be predicted with increases in the memory and processor speed of the computer.

It looks like the skepticism about superhuman intelligence is very human-centric though. After all, the knowledge a machine can acquire by using millions of cameras or microphones doesn't have to be limited by human vision or hearing. Machines can have their own views. Machines can integrate all the domain-specific knowledge like no human can, and, if it wants, the machine can add a module that has human-like intuitions as a legacy component. In any case, it will likely take many years for AGI to succeed, if it ever does. Regardless, the world's top-level researchers are working to develop AGI—this is not science fiction.

8.3 Proceed with care

As AI becomes more powerful and begins to do jobs without human help, we must be more careful in its use. Just like a fire used to cook a delicious meal can burn down a forest, AI can be used for benefit or for harm. Some safety issues should not be ignored. AI, especially its ANN components, can drive a car very well, for instance, but can't explain how it's doing the job. If that's the case, how can we guarantee it will always do a *good* job? If something goes wrong, who is to blame? The developer of the automobile? The developer of the AI modules? The designer of the simulation environment the ANN was trained on? The scientists who gathered the database the car was trained with?

Besides the safety issue, ethical issues may arise regarding how to treat AI robots, just like we have ethical issues with the treatment of animals. If AI are developed with more sensitive sensors and more autonomous control, will robots, at some point, start to have personalities and consciousness? If so, should we worry about respecting their opinions or their will for existence?

The world's most intelligent people, such as late physicist Stephen Hawking, entrepreneur and engineer Elon Musk, and Microsoft co-founder and entrepreneur Bill Gates have warned that AI may spell the end to human intelligence (Figure 8.6). In essence, when AI is more intelligent than we are, we can lose control of it, and we can no longer guarantee that AI will take actions we think of as good. Even if the AI has good intentions, what if it decides that it's best for the universe not to go along with human decisions? Some people, understandably, think we shouldn't worry that much about this. After all, we are the ones who make the programs. Why can't we just put in a safeguard? But, remember, at some point, AI will be able to outsmart us.

Many people also worry that AI may take away jobs (Figure 8.7). We already have unemployment problems in many parts of the world. There is no doubt that AI is already replacing some jobs. More terrifying, however, is this notion that, eventually, AI will be more intelligent than we are. Although it sounds like science fiction, if you analyze how much progress has been made and how likely it is we will continue making steady progress (despite opinions by Bentley and Pinker), you can predict that, sooner or later, AI will surpass human beings in terms of intelligence. If you think that AI can only take away repetitive jobs and can't take away jobs that require creativity, you're not totally correct. Generative ANNs can be trained in traditional arts and can then create samples of that art that it hasn't seen before. This has already been demonstrated to create interesting art and music.

Figure 8.6 Some serious thinkers have expressed concerned about the future impact of AI.

Figure 8.7 Computers are already replacing some jobs.

When AI surpasses human intelligence, our worth may not be measured by how smart we are, but by how wise we are. We should be smart enough to use AI, but, more than that, we should be wise enough to plan our future so that using AI will enrich our lives. Of course, there are always different views and opinions on this subject. Maybe we should stop developing AI, or maybe we should rest our future in the hands of AI—our new big boss. What do you think?

Figure 8.8 The future is in your hands.

Box 8.1 Three Laws of Robots

In his 1942 short story "Runaround," science-fiction novelist Isaac Asimov introduced the Three Laws of Robots:

1. A robot may not injure a human being or, through inaction, allow a human being to come to harm.
2. A robot must obey the orders given it by human beings except where such orders would conflict with the First Law.
3. A robot must protect its own existence as long as such protection does not conflict with the First or Second Laws.

Although the laws are old, they still look valid from an ethical point of view. But some people try to come up with laws that fit the current age and the future. Asimov's laws are about robotics, so they don't exactly apply to AI. As opposed to robots, whose existence is mainly in the physical domain, AI interacts with other AI and humans in more subtle ways. So, the term "harm" may be reinterpreted to include psychological, intellectual, and legal attacks. Can you come up with better rules? We must make sure AI won't harm us and will only be used to enhance our lives.

Questions

1. What is the name of a classical test of the sophistication level of AI as it makes conversations with humans?
2. What is the main reason that we can't download human knowledge or thoughts onto computers?
3. What is the main goal of Asimov's Three Laws of Robots?
4. What type of AI simulates human thought processes but isn't built to solve problems in particular fields?

Answers

1. Turing Test; 2. Because we don't know the neural code in the brain; 3. To protect humans; 4. Artificial general intelligence.

LIST OF FIGURES AND CREDITS

Chapter 1

Figure 1.1 Talking to a chatbot on the cell phone. (1) Looking at a cell phone. (Shutterstock 403782565, standard license). (2) Chatbot. (Shutterstock 650363986, standard license).

Figure 1.2 Computers are helping doctors to diagnose diseases. (Shutterstock 379665574, standard license).

Figure 1.3 Robots aren't science fiction anymore. A photograph by Tokumeigakarinoaoshima (Wikimedia Commons (WMC)) "File: SoftBank Pepper.JPG" 8/11/2014 (WMC, CC0 1.0).

Figure 1.4 Autonomous cars can drive themselves with little supervision from human drivers. (shutterstock 655226866, standard license).

Figure 1.5 A dialogue with Aristotle, a philosopher who developed a classical system of logic. (1) Aristotle: A photograph by Faustyna E. 5/12/2016 "File:Kopf des Aristoteles 1.jpg" (WMC, CC0 1.0). (2) Student cartoon: (shutterstock 421282873, standard license).

Figure 1.6 Application of Bayes' rule, one of the basic rules in statistics. Artist unknown 19c (WMC, public domain).

Figure 1.7 The basic elements making up your brain are called neurons. Graphics by selket (Wikimedia) 2/1/2007 "File: Neuron-no labels.png" (WMC, CC BY-SA 3.0).

Figure 1.8 Real (left) and artificial (right) neural networks. (1) Biological neural network. Photograph by Mark Miller 6/1/2005 "Mouse cingulate cortex neurons.jpg" (WMC, CC BY-SA 2.0). (2) Artificial neural network. Graphics by Zufzzi (WMC) date unknown "File: Neural network bottleneck achitecture2.svg" (WMC, public domain).

Chapter 2

Figure 2.1 Modeling the neurons. (1) Warren McCulloch. "WSMcCulloch_004.tiff" MIT Museum. Reproduced with permission. (2) Walter Pitts and Jerome Levin. Photograph by Iapx86

4/28/2006 (Wikipedia) "File: Lettvin Pitts.jpg" (WMC, CC BY-SA 3.0).

Figure 2.2 Frank Rosenblatt, creator of the perceptron. Photograph by anonymous, contributed 12/23/2017 "File: Rosenblatt 21.jpg" (WMC, CC BY-SA 4.0).

Figure 2.3 The Mark I perceptron. Photograph by National Museum of the U.S. Navy contributed 8/25/2015 "File: 330-PSA-80-60 (USN 710739) (20897323365).jpg" (WMC, public domain).

Figure 2.4 Backpropagation algorithm. (1) Cat. (Pixabay 1046402, CC0 1.0). (2) Neural network. (WMC, public domain).

Figure 2.5 Some of people who have contributed to the current resurgence in neural networks. (1) Geoffrey Hinton. Photograph by Eviatar Bach 5/20/2013 "File: Geoffrey Hinton at UBC.jpg" (WMC, CC BY-SA 3.0). (2) Yann LeCun. Photograph by Runner1928 (WMC) 10/20/2014 "File: Yann LeCun at the University of Minnesota.jpg" (WMC, CC BY-SA 3.0). (3) Yoshua Bengio. Photograph by Jérémy Barande 8/28/2017 "File: Yoshua Bengio (36468299790).jpg" (WMC, CC BY-SA 2.0). (4) Andrew Ng. Photograph by Steve Jurvetson, 2/27/2017 "File: Andrew Ng WSJ (2).jpg" (WMC, CC BY 2.0).

Figure 2.6 Graphics processing units can be used to speed up neural computation.
(Shutterstock 236188438, standard license).

Figure 2.7 Season changes in artificial intelligence. (1) Marvin Minsky. Photograph by Sethwoodworth 8/26/2008 (Wikipedia) "File: Marvin Minsky at OLPC.jpg" (WMC, CC BY-SA 3.0). (2) Snowman. (Pixabay 161228, CC0 1.0).

Chapter3

Figure 3.1 A teacher provides the correct answers in supervised learning. Teacher: (shutterstock 512126833, standard license).

Figure 3.2 A convoluted deep-learning network in supervised learning setting. (1) Dog: (pixabay669632, CC0 1.0). (2) Convolutional neural network: Graphics by aphex34 12/16/2015 (wikipedia) "File:Typical cnn.png", (WMC, CC BY-SA 4.0). (3) Teacher: (shutterstock 512126833, standard license)

Figure 3.3 A single layer artificial neural network.

Figure 3.4 Learning by the delta rule. Teacher: (shutterstock 512126833, standard license).

Figure 3.5 A picture generated by a generative neural network. Graphics created by Martin Thoma 1/14/2016 "File: Deep-dream-white-noise-0050.jpg" (WMC, CC0 1.0).

Chapter 4

Figure 4.1 ANNs can learn to group apples and oranges in unsupervised learning. (1) Apples and oranges. Photograph by Doudoulolita, 2/6/2010 "File: Pommes et oranges.jpg" (WMC, CC BY-SA 3.0). (2) Feature space. Graphics by Sigbert (WMC), 10/2/2011 "File: Swiss cmeans.svg" (WMC, CC BY-SA 3.0).

Figure 4.2 Teuvo Kohonen developed the self-organizing feature map (SOFM) model. (1) Teuvo Kohonen. Anonymous photographer, "File: Teuvo-Kohonen.jpg" (WMC, CC BY-SA 4.0). (2) Word map. Graphics by Denior (Wikipedia) 9/5/2013 "Self-organizing map cartography.jpg" (WMC, CC BY-SA 4.0).

Figure 4.3 The sensory map of the body in the brain. Graphics by OpenStax College 5/28/2013 "File: 1421 Sensory Homunculus.jpg" (WMC, CC BY-SA 3.0).

Figure 4.4 Hubel and Wiesel found visual columns in the cortex. (1) David Hubel. (ScienceSource SS2322490, ScienceSource license). (2) Torsten Wiesel. Photograph by Suawikicommons (WMC) 11/19/11 "File: Nobel Laureate Torsten Wiesel in 2011 Photo by Markus Marcetic for Young Academy of Sweden.jpg" (WMC, CC BY-SA 4.0). (3) Orientation column. Graphics by Albert Kok (WMC) 2/6/2007 "File: Module2.PNG" (WMC, public domain).

Figure 4.5 Self-organizing feature maps weight update.

Figure 4.6 Grouping of images. Cats and dogs. (Shutterstock 91233284, standard license).

Figure 4.7 Stephen Grossberg pioneered in psychophysical neural modeling. Photograph by Stephen Grossberg, 7/23/2016 "File: Stephen Grossberg in July, 2016.jpg" (WMC, CC BY-SA 4.0).

Figure 4.8 The ART1 network.

Figure 4.9 Autoencoder.

Chapter 5

Figure 5.1 Richard Sutton, one of the pioneers in reinforcement learning in artificial neural networks. Photograph by Steve Jurvetson, 10/27/2016 "File: Richard Sutton, October 27, 2016.jpg" (WMC, CC BY 2.0).

Figure 5.2 A diagram showing the components of reinforcement learning. (1) Mouse. (WPClipart, CC0). (2) Maze. (WPClipart, CC0). (3) Cheese. (Pixabay 1238395, CC0 1.0).

Figure 5.3 Reinforcement learning can be used to effectively learn computer games. Screen shot by Karawane_71 2/17/2015 "File: VideoOlympics.png" (WMC, public domain).

Figure 5.4 AI beats a Go champion. (1) Lee Sedol. Photograph captured by Cyberoro ORO, 10/2/2012 "File: Lee Se-dol 2012.jpg" (WMC, CC BY 3.0). (2) Go. (Shutterstock 558525793, standard license). (3) Computers. (Pixabay 1364652, CC0 1.0).

Figure 5.5 Robot can learn to stand up and run. Photograph by Mecian (WMC) 2010 "File: Robotics workshop 2.jpg" (WMC, public domain).

Figure 5.6 Simple V-learning after reaching state s. Mouse in maze in Figure 5.6–5.8 and 5.10–5.12: (Shutterstock 96727849, standard license).

Figure 5.7 V-learning with smoothing after reaching state s.

Figure 5.8 Temporal difference V-learning with smoothing after reaching state s, after which the mouse can reach state s'.

Figure 5.9 Reinforcement learning can be used to balance a pole. Photograph by ClarkH, 9/24/2006 "File: Balancer with wine 3.JPG" (WMC, CC BY-SA 3.0).

Figure 5.10 Simple Q-learning after taking action a and reaching state s.

Figure 5.11 Q-learning with smoothing after taking action a and reaching state s.

Figure 5.12 Temporal difference Q-learning with smoothing after taking action a and reaching state s, after which the mouse can take action a to reach state s'.

Figure 5.13 Self-driving car. Photograph by Denis Wolf (CaRINA project) 1/7/2013 "File: Carina2-lrm.jpg" (WMC, CC0 1.0).

Chapter 6

Figure 6.1 A voice-controlled personal assistant. (1) Girl. (Pixabay 511880, CC0). (2) Voice assistant. (Shutterstock 779412721, standard license).
Figure 6.2 A spectrogram of some German vowels. Graphics by Thomas Haslwanter 2/8/2012 "File: Vowel spectrogram.png" (WMC, CC BY-SA 3.0).
Figure 6.3 Word order in a miniature grammar.
Figure 6.4 A recurrent neural network.
Figure 6.5 A schematic representation of a recurrent artificial neural network and its unfolding to remove loops. Graphics by François Deloche 6/19/2017 "File: Recurrent neural network unfold.svg" (WMC, CC BY-SA 4.0).
Figure 6.6 The structure of long short-term memory.
Figure 6.7 Sequence-to-sequence conversion via a sentence representation. Based on graphics by François Deloche 6/19/2017 "File: Recurrent neural network unfold.svg" (WMC, CC BY-SA 4.0).
Figure 6.8 Conversation with a chatbot on the phone. (Shutterstock 494431294, standard license).

Chapter 7

Figure 7.1 A graphical model representing probabilistic relationships between five variables.
Figure 7.2 A schematic diagram explaining generative adversarial networks, a popular ANN model. Mona Lisa. (Pixabay 1124981 and 74050, CC0 1.0).
Figure 7.3 A neuron can compute more than just one big sum of weighted inputs. Dendrites. Graphics by ActiveDendrite (WMC) 10/14/2013 "File: From clusteron to sigmoidal neuron.png" (WMC, CC BY-SA 3.0).
Figure 7.4 A common structure of the surface of the human brain. The numbers indicate layer numbers from the surface of the cortex. Graphics by Mavavf (WMC) 10/13/2013 "File: Corteza cerebral.jpg" (WMC, CC BY-SA 3.0).

Figure 7.5 A computer simulation of activities of a small circuit in the rat brain. From Markram H, Muller E, Ramaswamy S, Reimann MW, Abdellah M, Sanchez CA, Ailamaki A, Alonso-Nanclares L, Antille N, Arsever S, Kahou GA. Reconstruction and simulation of neocortical microcircuitry. *Cell*. 2015;163(2):456–92,. Reproduced with permission.

Figure 7.6. EEG equipment and brain rhythms. (1) EEG preparation. (Shutterstock 494431294, standard license). (2) Brainwaves. Graphics by Pierre Etevenon (WMC) March 1987 "File: Analyse spectrale d'un EEG.jpg" (WMC, CC BY-SA 4.0).

Figure 7.7 Controlling a model car with the brain. Photograph by MirMish (WMC) 11/2/2015 "File: 544A4266.JPG" (WMC, CC BY-SA 4.0).

Figure 7.8 Hippocampus: (WPClipart, CC0).

Figure 7.9 Researchers who investigated navigation-related cells. (1) Nobel laurates. Photograph by Gunnar K. Hansen (NTNU) 12/6/2014 "File: Nobel prize laureates Moser and O'Keefe.jpg" (WMC, CC BY-SA 2.0). (2) Hippocampal place cells. Graphics by Stuartlayton (Wikipedia) 1/9/2013 "File: Place Cell Spiking Activity Example.png" (WMC, CC BY-SA 3.0).

Chapter 8

Figure 8.1 AI-assisted drug discovery. (Shutterstock 387764182, standard license).

Figure 8.2 A care robot. (Shutterstock 1113194153, standard license).

Figure 8.3 A robot that analyzes and responds to emotion. (1) A photograph by Tokumeigakarinoaoshima (Wikimedia) 8/11/2014 "File: SoftBank Pepper.JPG" (WMC, CC0 1.0). (2) A photograph by Alex Knight (Unsplash 199368, Unsplash license).

Figure 8.4 Robots can work in hazardous environments. Land Rover: A photograph by NASA/JPL/Cornell University, Maas Digital LLC Feb. 2013 "File: NASA Mars Rover.jpg" (WMC, public domain).

Figure 8.5 Research on quantum computing is accelerating. A photograph by IBM España 4/29/2018 (Flickr, public domain).

Figure 8.6 Some serious thinkers have expressed concerned about the future impact of AI. (1) Stephen Hawking. A photograph by [20100] (this is an uppercased username) 2006 "File: Stephen Hawking 050506.jpg" (WMC public domain) .(2) Elon Musk. A photograph by Author JD Lasica from Pleasanton, CA, US 11/7/2008 (CC BY 2.0). (3) Bill Gates. A photograph by World Economic Forum 1/26/2007 "File: Bill Gates in WEF, 2007.jpg" (WMC CC BY-SA 2.0).

Figure 8.7 Computers are already replacing some jobs. (Shutterstock 1154987062, standard license).

Figure 8.8 The future is in your hands. (Shutterstock 286990526, standard license).

Cover Design by Madeeha Shaikh, uses Adobe stock 187701690, extended license.

GLOSSARY

Algorithm: This is a list of operations for carrying out a task. For instance, a list of instructions for arranging a given set of numbers.

Android: An animal (including a human) augmented by machines or a robot augmented by biological components.

Artificial intelligence (AI): The capability of a machine to learn from experience and apply the knowledge in new situations.

Artificial general intelligence (AGI): Artificial Intelligence that solves problems across many areas, as opposed to Artificial Intelligence that solves only one kind of problems.

Artificial neural network (ANN): A set of artificial neurons interconnected with adjustable connection weights. By adjusting the connection weights, an ANN learns to produce the desired outputs for the given inputs.

Autonomous: Capable of functioning without help from outside sources including humans.

Autonomous car: A car that operates with little or no intervention from a human driver.

Chatbots: Computer programs that carry out conversations, typically through typing.

Cell: (1) A cellular phone. (2) The smallest structural and functional unit of a living organism that is enclosed by a thin membrane. Many cells can replicate themselves. For example, a biological neuron is a type of cell. (3) A nerve cell. See Neuron.

Central processing unit (CPU): An electronic circuit that performs arithmetic operations and data manipulations according to the program stored on a separate memory unit.

Column (Neural column): A group of cylindrical neurons that repeats horizontally in a neural tissue.

Electroencephalography (EEG): A method of recording line graphs of brain activities measured at different positions of the head.

Generative neural network: An artificial neural network that learns the hidden structures of the input data and later recreates output data that share the learned hidden structure.

Generative adversarial network (GAN): A generative neural network equipped with a discriminative neural network that compares generated and real data and trains the generator network to produce data indistinguishable from the real data.

Graphical model: A network of nodes (representing events and properties) connected with arrows (representing probabilistic relations between events and properties).

Graphics processing unit (GPU): This single-chip processor specializes in display functions. In AI, GPU rapidly performs two-dimensional (or higher) operations on large amounts of data required to run artificial neural networks.

Layer (Neural layer): A sheet-like group of neurons that is stacked up within a biological neural tissue or ANN. Each biological neural layer has a distinctive mixture of different neuron types.

Machine learning: An operation that makes it possible for a machine to process data in a flexible manner by analyzing the statistical characteristics of the data. Artificial neural networks can be defined as a type of machine learning.

Moore's law: An observation by Henry Moore that the number of transistors (elements in electronic circuits that perform amplification and gating) in a dense electronic circuit doubles every two years.

Neuron: A biological or an artificial unit that receives signals from other neurons, processes the signals, and sends out a signal.

Reinforcement learning: Learning methods that generate actions and utilize feedback from the environment to assess the outcome of the actions so that a better action is generated in the future.

Self-driving car: See Autonomous car.

Speech recognition: An operation that converts speech signals into a series of symbols.

Supervised learning: A learning method by providing both inputs and desirable outputs.

Synapse: A connection through which a signal is transmitted from one neuron to another neuron.

Unsupervised learning: A learning method that solely relies on exposure to input data.

Voice recognition: See Speech recognition.

REFERENCES

1. Original books and papers

The following are original books and papers referred to in this book. They may not be easy reads, but they are classics and there is nothing like reading classics.

[1] Carpenter GA, Grossberg S. A massively parallel architecture for a self-organizing neural pattern recognition machine. *Computer Vision, Graphics, and Image Processing.* 1987;37:54–115.

[2] Hebb DO. *The Organization of Behavior.* New York: John Wiley and Sons, Inc.; 1949.

[3] Hubel DH, Wiesel TN. Sequence regularity and geometry of orientation columns in the monkey striate cortex. *Journal of Comparative Neurology.* 1974;158(3):267–93.

[4] Kohonen T. Self-organized formation of topologically correct feature maps. *Biological cybernetics.* 1982;43(1):59-69.

[5] LeCun Y, Bengio Y, Hinton G. Deep learning. *nature.* 2015;521(7553):436.

[6] McCulloch W, Pitts WA. Logical calculus of the ideas immanent in nervous activity. *Bulletin of Mathematical Biophysics.* 1943;5:115–133.

[7] Rosenblatt, F. The perceptron: a probabilistic model for information storage and organization in the brain. *Psychological Review.* 1958;65(6):386–408.

[8] Sutton RS. Learning to predict by the methods of temporal differences. *Machine learning.* 1988;3(1):9-44.

[9] Turing AM. On computable numbers, with an application to the Entscheidungsproblem. *Proceedings of the London Mathematical Society.* 1937;2(1):230–65.

2. Further reading

The following are college level textbooks on artificial neural networks for further study.

- Goodfellow I, Bengio Y, Courville A. *Deep Learning.* Cambridge: MIT Press; 2016.
- Haykin SS. *Neural Networks and Learning Machines.* Upper Saddle River: Pearson; 2009.
- Bishop CM, *Pattern Recognition and Machine Learning.* New York: Springer-Verlag; 2006.

3. Special mention

This is a lucid and charming book written by an 11-year-old boy and his father.

Lane K. *When Computers Become Human: A Kid's Guide to the Future of Artificial Intelligence.* Mount San Antonio College Philosophy Group, 2017.

INDEX

ABOUT THE AUTHOR

Michiro Negishi worked on neural networks at Mitsubishi Electric in Japan before coming to the United States to earn a Ph.D. in neuroscience from Boston University. He has worked on the neural-network simulation of children's language acquisition at Rutgers University and on brain imaging at Yale University. Currently, Michiro Negishi is the CEO of Neuroverb, a company that specializes in research and education on neural networks.

Made in the USA
Lexington, KY
13 March 2019